# Ready, Set... GRAMMAR! ™

**A Beginning Grammar Program for Non-Readers**

**Mark Barrett
Rosemary Huisingh
Linda Zachman
and the staff of
LinguiSystems**

D1205347

**LinguiSystems®**

LinguiSystems, Inc.
3100 4th Avenue
East Moline, IL 61244

**1-800-PRO IDEA
1-800-776-4332**

| Skill Area: | Grammar |
| Interest Level: | Preschool thru 3rd grade |

Copyright © 1988 LinguiSystems, Inc.

Limited Reproduction Allowed

LinguiSystems grants to individual teachers and other professionals the limited right to reproduce and distribute copies of these worksheets for non-commercial, face-to-face individual, group or classroom instruction. All copies must include LinguiSystems' copyright notice.

Reproduction and distribution of these worksheets for an entire school, school system or group of professionals is strictly prohibited.

ISBN 1-55999-067-8

## About the Authors

Mark, Rosemary, and Linda are all publishing speech-language pathologists by day and practicing parents at night.   They are lovers of language, learning, laughing, and children — not necessarily in that order.   Among their special educational offspring are numerous books (*Activities for Children Involving Everyday Vocabulary-ACHIEV, Teaching Vocabulary Worksheets, Blooming Language Arts, Thinking To Go*), several tests (including the *Test Of Problem Solving-TOPS* and *The WORD Test*), and even (gasp!) an educational game (*Language Land*).   Mark, Rosemary, and Linda hope that the fun, interactive pages of *Ready, Set, Grammar!* inspire your language-learners to *enjoy* their way to grammar and syntax success.

Four speech-language pathologists of LinguiSystems' staff contributed mightily to this writing project:   Carolyn Blagden, Barbara Walter, Kamala Simonton, and Jane Orman. Their creative skills, astute problem solving, and fresh ideas helped make *Ready, Set, Grammar!* a reality.

February 1988

---

For you and your students--
the best language, learning, and thinking materials.
LinguiSystems' promise to you.

We welcome your comments on *Ready, Set...Grammar!* and other LinguiSystems products. Please send your comments to Molly Lyle, Editorial Manager.

---

8188552

# Table of Contents

# Foreword

*. . .a person try talkin' an' him havin' trouble puttin' all the word and sentence 'gether, hims friends gonna not understan' him. . .'cuz the person speech all mess up, him not wanna talk inside class. . .last time him answer a question, all hims classmate was. . .*

The little words. The ends of words. The order of words. Oh, how these "small" pieces of our language play such a big role in the communication puzzle. The child who never learns the rules, let alone the *art,* of grammar and syntax, may be destined to a lifetime of inarticulate, imprecise speech.

Enter *Ready, Set, Grammar!* stage left. With this series of interactive grammar programs, you'll help your young language-learners understand and use the structures of oral language. Through progressive and systematic steps, your students learn to organize and expand their speech grammatically. And their learning is enhanced through active, hands-on, *doing* activities as a part of each lesson.

So, if your 4- through 10-year-old students have oral grammar skills only slightly better than Morse code, keep on reading. *Ready, Set, Grammar!* is perfect for your youngsters. . .and you!

MB
RH
LZ

5

# Introduction

How can the oral grammar needs of language-deficient children best be addressed? That's the question we faced when we began creating *Ready, Set, Grammar!* We decided that the program needed to be comprehensive, systematic, flexible, interactive, and fun. Sounds like a good prescription for all instruction, right?

So how comprehensive is *Ready, Set, Grammar!*? Twelve of the most frequently misused grammatical structures are addressed, ranging from verbs to plurals and from prepositions to pronouns. In addition, the structures represent many of the early developing language structures according to Roger Brown's research.[1] The twelve structures are presented in a logical, developmental sequence, and are described below.

*Present Progressive* Using *is verb+ing* and *are verb+ing* constructions is frequently difficult for the language-deficient child. Omission of the *to be* verb and subject-verb agreement errors are commonly heard.

*Past Progressive* The *was verb+ing* and *were verb+ing* combinations are similarly troublesome for children with oral grammar problems. Errors such as "They was driving fast," and "My sister babysitting last night," are frequent.

*Past Regular* Inclusion of the *-ed* past tense verb ending is one of the most common targets of grammar instruction. Children must also learn when a /t/ or /d/ ending sound is added (e.g., "talked" or "smiled").

*Past Irregular* The various classes of irregular verbs that form their past tenses without *-ed* endings are problems for children with language disorders, as well as for students developing language normally. An array of common irregular verbs (e.g., "sleep-slept," "eat-ate," "run-ran") is presented in *Ready, Set Grammar!*

*Third Person Singular* Many children with oral grammar and syntax difficulties fail to add the *-s* ending to present tense, third person singular verbs ("The boy draw a picture," instead of "The boy draws a picture."). Sometimes the third person singular is formed by the addition of another syllable (/əz/ as in "dances"), and other times it is simply formed by adding an /s/ or /z/ ending sound (e.g., "drinks" or "reads").

*Future* Skillful use of *will + verb* to denote the future tense requires children to discard previous, less mature constructions of "gonna" and "going to." In *Ready, Set, Grammar!,* the future tense is contrasted visually and verbally with the present progressive verb tense.

---

[1]Brown, R. *A First Language* Harvard University Press (1973).

*Prepositions*   The following spatial prepositions are taught in *Ready, Set, Grammar!*:  *in, on, over, under, next to, between, behind,* and *in front of.*   For optimal success, these concepts are presented and contrasted in pairs.

*Regular Plurals*   Indicating the plural condition of nouns by adding *-s* or *-es* is necessary for accurate, clear communication.   In learning this structure, children must learn whether an /s/ or /z/ ending sound is necessary (e.g., "plates" or "dogs").

*Irregular Plurals*   Some nouns form their plurals rather illogically and compound the problems of the young language-learner.   A broad sampling of irregular plurals (e.g., "man-men," "sheep-sheep," "knife-knives") is covered in *Ready, Set, Grammar!*

*Possessive Nouns*   Children with language-learning difficulties often omit the *-s* or *-es* endings on nouns needed to show possession or ownership.   As with regular plural formation, some nouns form their possessives with the addition of an /s/ or /z/ ending sound (e.g., "Jeff's" or "the dog's").

*Possessive Pronouns*   Using *his, her, its,* and *their* frequently poses problems for students with oral grammar deficiencies.   These children may overgeneralize their use of the possessive *-s* ending and form combinations such as "hers homework" and "thems house."

*Subjective Pronouns*   The young language-learner often confuses and substitutes personal pronouns used as objects (*him, her it,* and *them*) with their counterparts — personal pronouns used as subjects (*he, she, it* and *they*).   This confusion results in errors such as "Him hit me," or "Them are no good."

The programs in *Ready, Set, Grammar!* are systematic and progress in small, success-oriented steps.   The child's proficiency for each structure is initially assessed through expressive and receptive pretests.   For these tasks, the child first describes what he sees in a pictured scene.   Then, he points or performs another specified nonverbal task during the receptive pretesting.   The instructional parts of the *Ready, Set, Grammar!* programs are described below:

*Auditory Bombardment*   The student listens carefully as you point to each picture on the worksheet and say a word or phrase containing the target structure.

*Auditory Discrimination*   After you say a word or phrase containing the target structure, the student points to the corresponding picture on the worksheet.

*Word/Phrase Repetition*   As you point to a picture, the student imitates your verbal model of a word or phrase containing the target structure.

*Word/Phrase Production*   When you point to a picture and ask a question, the student spontaneously says a word or phrase with the target structure.

*Sentence Repetition*   As you point to a picture, the student imitates your verbal model of a short sentence containing the target structure.

*Sentence Production*   When you point to a picture and ask a question, the student spontaneously says a short sentence containing the target structure.

*Expanded Sentence Repetition*   As you point to a picture and ask a question, the student imitates your verbal model of an expanded sentence containing the target structure.

*Expanded Sentence Production*   When you point to a picture and ask a question, the student spontaneously says an expanded sentence containing the target structure.

*Carryover*   The student spontaneously describes what he sees in a pictured scene, using the target structure as he speaks.

The instructional program is concluded with a posttest that gives you further information about the child's proficiency in spontaneously using the target structure in his speech.

Although a consistent program is followed throughout *Ready, Set, Grammar!*, don't be misled.   This program is definitely meant to be flexible.   Program steps can be skipped if they don't seem necessary.   Because the worksheets are paired, it is easy to conduct the program with two worksheets and eight picture examples of the structure at the same time.   The pictured scenes of the pretest, carryover, and posttest can be interchanged and used more than once.   In general, feel free to add or modify the program content according to the needs of your students.

We believe that the best instruction is interactive instruction.   Children learn best when they can actively participate and share.   That's why you'll find nifty To Do activities on every page of *Ready, Set, Grammar!*   As your students cut and paste, assemble and create, you can enhance and expand those priceless "teachable moments."   You'll be thrilled at how successful and inspired your language-learners will be.

As you may have guessed by now, *Ready, Set, Grammar!* is truly fun-filled instruction. Delightful pictures, success-filled program steps, and engaging To Do activities all give you the grammar ammunition you need for session after enjoyable session.   Just turn the pages and turn your language-learners into language-achievers.

# Ready, Set, Grammar!
## Progress Chart

grammatical structure        student's name

Trials

| Program Step | 1 | 2 | 3 | 4 | 5 | 6 | 7 | 8 | 9 | 10 |
|---|---|---|---|---|---|---|---|---|---|---|
| Pretest, Expressive | | | | | | | | | | |
| Pretest, Receptive | | | | | | | | | | |
| Auditory Bombardment | | | | | | | | | | |
| Auditory Discrimination | | | | | | | | | | |
| Word/Phrase Repetition | | | | | | | | | | |
| Word/Phrase Production | | | | | | | | | | |
| Sentence Repetition | | | | | | | | | | |
| Sentence Production | | | | | | | | | | |
| Expanded Sentence Repetition | | | | | | | | | | |
| Expanded Sentence Production | | | | | | | | | | |
| Carryover | | | | | | | | | | |
| Posttest | | | | | | | | | | |

Use this Progress Chart to record the student's performance on a grammatical structure over several trials. Enter the date of the trial in the shaded section of the row of the appropriate program step. Then, enter the percentage correct for the program step in the unshaded portion of the row.

Name _____

11

## Worksheet 1: At the Park

### Pretest Directions: Expressive

Look at this picture. It shows people doing things. Tell me what all of these people are doing. (If the child has difficulty, point to each picture and say,) Tell me about this one. (Continue until the child describes all the action with sentences such as:)

1. The people <u>are</u> <u>walking</u>.

2. The woman <u>is</u> <u>running</u>.

3. The children <u>are</u> <u>playing</u>.

4. The baby <u>is</u> <u>sleeping</u>.

5. The people <u>are</u> <u>eating</u>.

6. The girl <u>is</u> <u>crying</u>.

7. The artist <u>is</u> <u>painting</u>.

8. The man <u>is</u> <u>sitting</u>.

### Pretest Directions: Receptive

Materials: red, green, yellow, blue, purple, orange, black, and pink crayons

Let's practice listening carefully. Look at your worksheet. There are many people doing things. I will talk about each person. I will also tell you what to do on your worksheet.

1. Listen. Draw a red X on what I say. The people are walking.

2. Listen. Draw a green X on what I say. The woman is running.

3. Listen. Draw a yellow X on what I say. The children are playing.

4. Listen. Draw a blue X on what I say. The baby is sleeping.

5. Listen. Draw a purple X on what I say. The people are eating.

6. Listen. Draw an orange X on what I say. The girl is crying.

7. Listen. Draw a black X on what I say. The artist is painting.

8. Listen. Draw a pink X on what I say. The man is sitting.

Good listening!

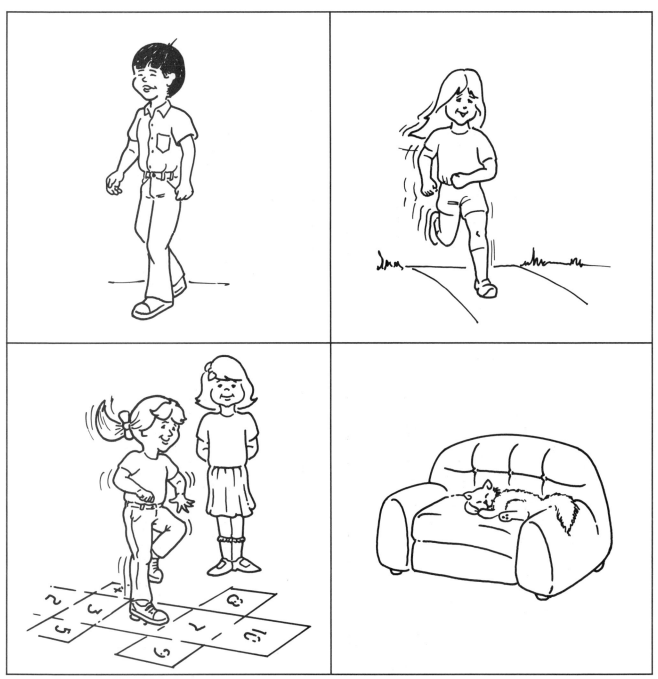

**Auditory Bombardment**  Listen carefully. (Name the actions as you slowly point to each picture.)
  walking
  running
  playing
  sleeping

**Auditory Discrimination**  Listen to what I say. Then, point to the picture I talk about.  (Ask about the pictures at random.)
  Show me who is . . . walking.
                                    running.
                                    playing.
                                    sleeping.

**To Do Activity**  Cut these pictures apart and mount them on cards.  Play a game of charades with the child.  Take turns acting out one of the cards and having the other person point to the correct picture.

PRESENT PROGRESSIVE                    13

Name _____

**Auditory Bombardment**   Listen carefully.   (Name the actions as you slowly point to each picture.)
   eating
   crying
   painting
   sitting

**Auditory Discrimination**   Listen to what I say. Then, point to the picture I talk about.   (Ask about the pictures at random.)
   Show me who is . . . eating.
                           crying.
                           painting.
                           sitting.

**To Do Activity**   Cut these pictures apart and mount them on pieces of construction paper.   Have the child choose a piece and add it to the train if he identifies the picture correctly.

14

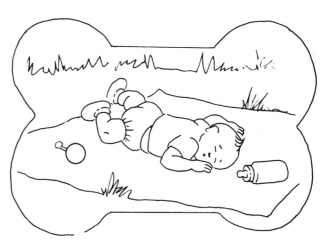

**Word Repetition**   Say what I say.   (Point to each picture as you say:)
    walking
    running
    playing
    sleeping

**Word Production**   (Point to each picture and ask,) What is/are the ___ doing?   (The child answers with the appropriate response of:)
    walking
    running
    playing
    sleeping

**To Do Activity**   Cut these pictures apart and mount them on pieces of construction paper.   Make a dog or use a stuffed dog to go with the bones.   Let the child pick a bone and give it to the dog if she identifies the picture correctly.

Name _____

**Word Repetition** Say what I say. (Point to each picture as you say:)

    eating
    crying
    painting
    sitting

**Word Production** (Point to each picture and ask,) What is/are the ___ doing? (The child answers with the appropriate response of:)

    eating
    crying
    painting
    sitting

**To Do Activity** Cut these pictures apart and trace the outline of each person on another sheet of paper. Let the child match the outlines with the appropriate pictures if he can label the actions correctly.

16

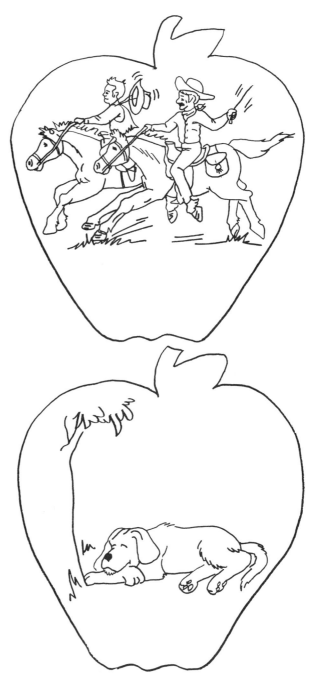

**Sentence Repetition**   Say what I say.   (Point to each picture as you say:)
   The man is walking.
   The horses are running.
   The girl is sitting.
   The dog is sleeping.

**Sentence Production**   (Point to each picture and ask,) What is/are the ___ doing?   (The child responds with sentences such as:)
   The man <u>is</u> <u>walking</u>.
   The horses <u>are</u> <u>running</u>.
   The girl <u>is</u> <u>sitting</u>.
   The dog <u>is</u> <u>sleeping</u>.

**To Do Activity**   Draw the outline of a tree.   Then, cut these pictures apart and mount them on pieces of construction paper.   Have the child select an apple and add it to the tree for each picture she describes correctly in a sentence.

Name _____

**Sentence Repetition**  Say what I say.  (Point to each picture as you say:)
  The cows are eating.
  The woman is painting.
  The boy is crying.
  The children are playing.

**Sentence Production**  (Point to each picture and ask,) What is/are the ___ doing?  (The child responds with sentences such as:)
  The cows <u>are</u> <u>eating</u>.
  The woman <u>is</u> <u>painting</u>.
  The boy <u>is</u> <u>crying</u>.
  The children <u>are</u> <u>playing</u>.

**To Do Activity**  Have the child make a background scene for each picture from construction paper.  Cut out the pictures on this worksheet and glue them onto the appropriate scenes.  Then, have the child describe each scene she has created.

18

**Expanded Sentence Repetition**   Say what I say.
(Point to each picture as you say:)
   The girl is walking across the street.
   The boy is running to the bus.
   The child is sleeping in the stroller.
   The girls are playing basketball.

**Expanded Sentence Production**   (Point to one of
the pictures and ask,) What is/are the ____ doing?
(The child responds with expanded sentences
such as:)
   The girl is walking across the street.
   The boy is running to the bus.
   The child is sleeping in the stroller.
   The girls are playing basketball.

**To Do Activity**   Cut these pictures apart and mount them on pieces of colored construction paper.   Lay the
pictures in front of the child and have her close her eyes while you cover up one of the pictures.   Then,
have her open her eyes and use a correct sentence to describe the picture you are covering up.

19

**Expanded Sentence Repetition**   Say what I say.
(Point to each picture as you say:)
   The girl is crying beside the tree.
   The men are painting the building.
   The girl is sitting on the swing.
   The boys are eating apples.

**Expanded Sentence Production**   (Point to each
picture and ask,) What is/are the ___ doing?   (The
child responds with expanded sentences such as:)
   The girl is crying beside the tree.
   The men are painting the building.
   The girl is sitting on the swing.
   The boys are eating apples.

**To Do Activity**   Cut these pictures apart and paste them on cards.   Select one of the cards and say what
the person is doing.   Then ask, "What else is ___ doing?"   See how many different complete sentences
the child can give for each picture.

20

**Worksheet 6: After School**

## Worksheet 6: After School

**Carryover Directions**

Tell me about this picture. (If the child has difficulty, point to one of the action sequences and ask,) What is/are the ___ doing? (Continue with the task until the child describes all the action with sentences such as:)

1. The girl <u>is</u> <u>walking</u> across the street.

2. The boy <u>is</u> <u>running</u> to the bus.

3. The child <u>is</u> <u>sleeping</u> in the stroller.

4. The girls <u>are</u> <u>playing</u> basketball.

5. The girl <u>is</u> <u>crying</u> beside the tree.

6. The men <u>are</u> <u>painting</u> the school.

7. The girl <u>is</u> <u>sitting</u> on the swing.

8. The boys <u>are</u> <u>eating</u> apples.

**To Do Activity**

Have the child bring in photos of his family. Use complete sentences to talk about what his family members are doing/wearing, etc. If you are working on "<u>I</u> am verbing," use pictures of the child himself.

**Worksheet 7: In the Backyard**

23

# Worksheet 7:   In the Backyard

## Posttest Directions

Here are some pictures.   Tell me what the people and the animals are doing.   Tell me all about them.   (If the child has difficulty, point to one of the action sequences and ask,) What is/are the ___ doing?   (Continue until the child describes all the action with sentences such as:)

1.   The woman <u>is</u> <u>talking</u> to the man.

2.   The man <u>is</u> <u>cooking</u> on the grill.

3.   The little boy <u>is</u> <u>riding</u> his big wheel.

4.   The rabbits <u>are</u> <u>hopping</u> across the yard.

5.   The girls <u>are</u> <u>diving</u> into the pool.

6.   The woman <u>is</u> <u>digging</u> in the garden.

7.   The girl <u>is</u> <u>climbing</u> a tree.

8.   The babies <u>are</u> <u>crawling</u> to the garden.

## To Do Activity

Cut pictures apart from comic strips and have the children resequence the pictures and talk about the actions using complete sentences.

## Worksheet 1A: In the Backyard

Use this scene with the scene on the next page.

25

**Worksheet 1B:   In the Backyard**

Use this scene with the scene on the previous page.

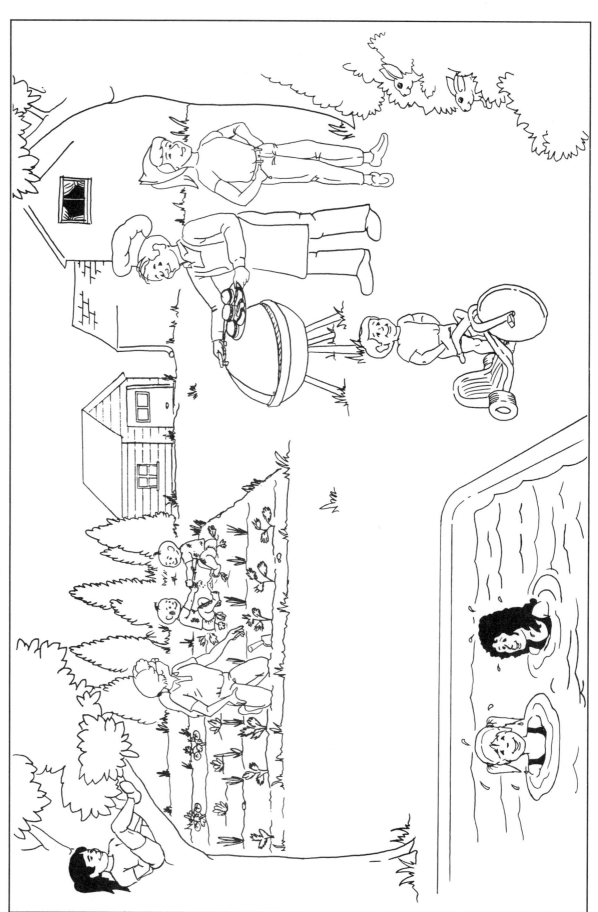

26

# Worksheets 1A and 1B: In the Backyard

## Pretest Directions: Expressive

Look at these two pictures. The first picture shows people and animals doing things. In the second picture, they are finished doing these things. Tell me what each person and animal was doing. (If the child has difficulty, provide a question prompt. For example, point to the man cooking and say,) Here, the man is cooking. (Then, point to the man in the next picture and say,) Now, he is done. What was he doing? (The child responds, *The man was cooking.* Continue until the child uses the past progressive in sentences such as:)

1.  The man was cooking.

2.  The boy was riding.

3.  The rabbits were hopping.

4.  The girls were diving.

5.  The babies were crawling.

6.  The girl was climbing.

7.  The woman was digging.

8.  The woman was talking.

## Pretest Directions: Receptive

Materials: red, green, yellow, blue, purple, orange, black, and pink crayons

Let's practice listening carefully. Look at your worksheets. I will talk about what each person or animal was doing. I will also tell you what to do on your worksheets. (Present items randomly from both worksheets.)

1.  Listen. Draw a red line above who is/was cooking.

2.  Listen. Draw a green line above who is/was riding.

3.  Listen. Draw a yellow line above what are/were hopping.

4.  Listen. Draw a blue line above who are/were diving.

5.  Listen. Draw a purple line above who are/were crawling.

6.  Listen. Draw an orange line above who is/was climbing.

7.  Listen. Draw a black line above who is/was digging.

8.  Listen. Draw a pink line above who is/was talking.

Good listening!

**Auditory Bombardment**   Listen carefully.
(Describe the actions, stressing the past progressive
as you slowly point to each picture.)
    The children are cooking.   Now they're done.
        The children were cooking.
    The cowboy is riding.   Now, he's done.
        The cowboy was riding.

**Auditory Discrimination**   Listen to what I say.
Then, point to the picture I talk about.   (Describe
the pictures at random.)
    The children are cooking.
    The children were cooking.
    The cowboy is riding.
    The cowboy was riding.

**To Do Activity**   Make an action mobile.   First, have the child color each person.   Then, cut the pictures
apart, paste them on pieces of colored construction paper, and tie a piece of yarn to each one.   If the child
points to the picture you describe, let her tie it to a hanger to make the mobile.

28

**Auditory Bombardment**    Listen carefully.
(Describe the actions, stressing the past progressive as you slowly point to each picture.)
    The kangaroo is hopping.    Now, it's done.
        The kangaroo was hopping.
    The boy is diving.    Now, he's done.
        The boy was diving.

**Auditory Discrimination**    Listen to what I say.
Then, point to the picture I talk about.    (Describe the pictures at random.)
    The kangaroo is hopping.
    The kangaroo was hopping.
    The boy is diving.
    The boy was diving.

**To Do Activity**    Cut these pictures apart and mount them on pieces of tag board.    Have the child glue yarn around the outside edge of the pictures for frames.    Then, see if he can point to the pictures you describe.

29

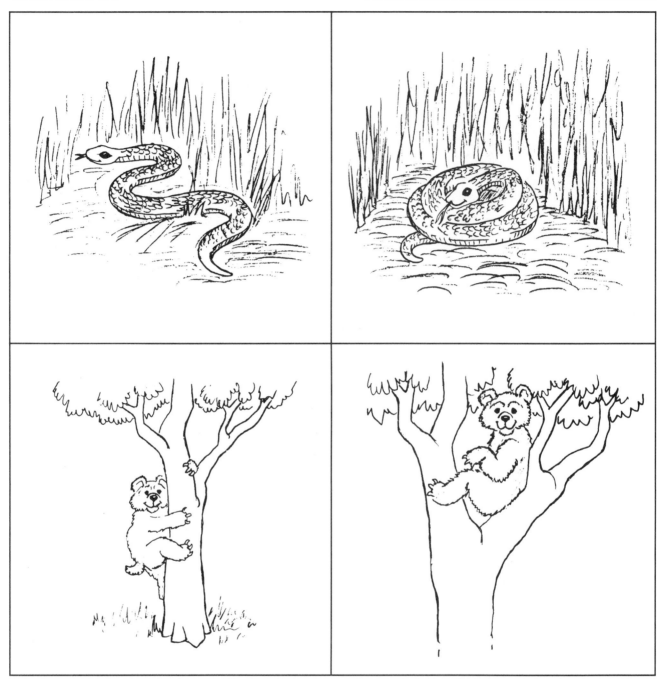

**Auditory Bombardment**   Listen carefully.
(Describe the actions, stressing the past progressive as you slowly point to each picture.)
   The snake is crawling.   Now, it's done.
     The snake was crawling.
   The bear is climbing.   Now, it's done.
     The bear was climbing.

**Auditory Discrimination**   Listen to what I say.
Then, point to the picture I talk about.   (Describe the pictures at random.)
   The snake is crawling.
   The snake was crawling.
   The bear is climbing.
   The bear was climbing.

**To Do Activity**   Have the child pretend to be each of the animals on this page.   Describe each of the pictures in the order listed and have her act them out.

30

Name _____

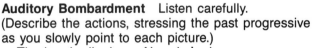

**Auditory Bombardment**   Listen carefully.
(Describe the actions, stressing the past progressive as you slowly point to each picture.)
 The boy is digging.   Now, he's done.
  The boy was digging.
 The boys are talking.   Now, they're done.
  The boys were talking.

**Auditory Discrimination**   Listen to what I say.
Then, point to the picture I talk about.   (Describe the pictures at random.)
 The boy is digging.
 The boy was digging.
 The boys are talking.
 The boys were talking.

**To Do Activity**   Cut these pictures apart and mount them on pieces of colored construction paper.   Draw an outline of a Christmas tree for the ornaments.   If the child points to the picture you describe, let him paste that picture on the tree.

**Sentence Repetition**   (Point to each picture as you say:)

   Listen.   The man is cooking.   Now, he's done.
     Say what I say:   The man was cooking.
   Listen.   The boy is riding.   Now, he's done.
     Say what I say:   The boy was riding.

**Sentence Production**   (Point to each picture and ask,) What is/was the ___ doing?   (The child responds with sentences such as:)

   The man <u>is cooking</u>.
   The man <u>was cooking</u>.
   The boy <u>is riding</u>.
   The boy <u>was riding</u>.

**To Do Activity**   Describe the pictures to the child at random.   Have her color the present progressive verbs one color, and the past progressive verbs another.   Then, have her describe the pictures using correct sentences.

**Sentence Repetition**   (Point to each picture as you say:)

> Listen.   The rabbits are hopping.   Now, they're done.   Say what I say:   The rabbits were hopping.
>
> Listen.   The girls are diving.   Now, they're done.   Say what I say:   The girls were diving.

**Sentence Production**   (Point to each picture and ask,)   What are/were the ___ doing?   (The child responds with sentences such as:)

> The rabbits <u>are</u> <u>hopping</u>.
> The rabbits <u>were</u> <u>hopping</u>.
> The girls <u>are</u> <u>diving</u>.
> The girls <u>were</u> <u>diving</u>.

**To Do Activity**   Cut the pictures apart to make four jigsaw puzzle pieces.   Have the child put the pieces back together on a piece of cardboard.   Glue the pieces on the cardboard to make sure they stay together. Let the child color the picture if he describes it using a correct sentence.

**Sentence Repetition**   (Point to each picture as you say:)
   Listen.   The babies are crawling.   Now, they're done.   Say what I say:   The babies were crawling.
   Listen.   The girl is climbing.   Now, she's done.   Say what I say:   The girl was climbing.

**Sentence Production**   (Point to each picture and ask,) What is/was the ___ doing? / What are/were the ___ doing?   (The child responds with sentences such as:)
   The babies <u>are crawling</u>.
   The babies <u>were crawling</u>.
   The girl <u>is climbing</u>.
   The girl <u>was climbing</u>.

**To Do Activity**   Have the child imagine what might happen next in each of these sequences.   Then, have her draw her own version of what the following frame for each action might be.   Have her describe both new sequences of pictures using correct sentences.

PAST PROGRESSIVE                              34

**Sentence Repetition**   (Point to each picture as you say:)

Listen.   The woman is digging.   Now, she's done.   Say what I say:   The woman was digging.

Listen.   The woman is talking.   Now, she's done.   Say what I say:   The woman was talking.

**Sentence Production**   (Point to each picture and ask,) What is/was the ___ doing?   (The child responds with sentences such as:)

The woman is digging.
The woman was digging.
The woman is talking.
The woman was talking.

**To Do Activity**   Cut these pictures apart and mount them on pieces of construction paper.   Decorate a shoebox to look like a zoo.   Let the child pick an animal and put it in the zoo if he can describe the picture correctly in a sentence.

**Expanded Sentence Repetition**   (Point to each picture as you say:)

   Listen.   The woman is cooking hot dogs over the camp fire.   Now, she's done.   Say what I say: The woman was cooking hot dogs over the camp fire.

   Listen.   The boy is riding his bike on the path. Now, he's done.   Say what I say:   The boy was riding his bike on the path.

**Expanded Sentence Production**   (Point to each picture and ask,)  What is/was the _____ doing? (The child responds with expanded sentences such as:)

   The woman <u>is</u> <u>cooking</u> hot dogs over the camp fire.
   The woman <u>was</u> <u>cooking</u> hot dogs over the camp fire.
   The boy <u>is</u> <u>riding</u> his bike on the path.
   The boy <u>was</u> <u>riding</u> his bike on the path.

**To Do Activity**   Cut these pictures apart and mount them on colored pieces of tag board.   Make a mailbox out of a shoebox and let the child mail a letter if she describes the picture using a correct expanded sentence.

36

**Expanded Sentence Repetition**  (Point to each picture as you say:)

    Listen.   The frogs are hopping on the rocks. Now, they're done.   Say what I say:   The frogs were hopping on the rocks.

    Listen.   The boy is diving into the pond.   Now, he's done.   Say what I say:   The boy was diving into the pond.

**Expanded Sentence Production**   (Point to each picture and ask,)  What is/was the ___ doing? / What are/were the ___ doing?   (The child responds with expanded sentences such as:)

    The frogs <u>are</u> <u>hopping</u> on the rocks.
    The frogs <u>were</u> <u>hopping</u> on the rocks.
    The boy <u>is</u> <u>diving</u> into the pond.
    The boy <u>was</u> <u>diving</u> into the pond.

**To Do Activity**   Have the child color the pictures on this worksheet, cut them apart, and put them on a bulletin board in the correct sequence.   Then, have the child describe the different actions in complete sentences.

**Expanded Sentence Repetition**  (Point to each picture as you say:)

   Listen.   The boy is crawling to his father.   Now, he's done.   Say what I say:  The boy was crawling to his father.
   Listen.   The girl is climbing a tree.   Now, she's done.   Say what I say:  The girl was climbing a tree.

**Expanded Sentence Production**  (Point to each picture and ask,)  What is/was the ____ doing? (The child responds with expanded sentences such as:)

   The boy is crawling to his father.
   The boy was crawling to his father.
   The girl is climbing a tree.
   The girl was climbing a tree.

**To Do Activity**  Cut the pictures apart and paste them onto separate pieces of paper.   Have the child make two storybooks by putting the pictures in the correct sequence and stapling them together.   He can add other pages to the books to make longer stories.   Add a cover with a title and the child's name.   Then, have the child "read" the story to you, using complete sentences.

Name _____

**Expanded Sentence Repetition**  (Point to each picture as you say:)

    Listen.  The girls are digging a hole.  Now, they're done.  Say what I say:  The girls were digging a hole.

    Listen.  The father is talking to the mother. Now, he's done.  Say what I say:  The father was talking to the mother.

**Expanded Sentence Production**  (Point to each picture and ask,)  What is/was the ___ doing? / What are/were the ___ doing?  (The child responds with expanded sentences such as:)

    The girls <u>are</u> <u>digging</u> a hole.
    The girls <u>were</u> <u>digging</u> a hole.
    The father <u>is talking</u> to the mother.
    The father <u>was</u> <u>talking</u> to the mother.

**To Do Activity**  Cut these pictures apart and place them face down on the table.  Give the child a winter scene, either from a magazine or drawn by the child.  Then, have the child pick a picture.  If she describes it using a correct expanded sentence, let her paste it on the winter background.  For extra fun, let her complete the snowman by drawing the arms and scarf when she has all the pieces of the snowman together.

         39         

**Worksheet 5A:   At the Pond**

Use this scene with the scene on the next page.

40

Name _____

Use this scene with the scene on the previous page.

41

## Worksheets 5A and 5B:  At the Pond

### Carryover Directions

Look at these two pictures.   The first picture shows people and animals doing things.   In the second picture they are finished doing these things.   Tell me what each person and animal was doing.   (If the child has difficulty, provide a question prompt.   For example, point to the mother cooking and say,) Here, the mother is cooking hot dogs.   (Then, point to the woman in the next picture and say,) Now, she is done.   What was she doing?   (The child responds, *The mother was cooking hot dogs.*   Continue until the child uses the past progressive in sentences such as:)

1. The mother <u>was</u> <u>cooking</u> hot dogs.

2. The boy <u>was</u> <u>riding</u> his bike on the path.

3. The frogs <u>were</u> <u>hopping</u> on the rocks.

4. The boy <u>was</u> <u>diving</u> into the pond.

5. The boy <u>was</u> <u>crawling</u> to his father.

6. The girl <u>was</u> <u>climbing</u> the tree.

7. The girls <u>were</u> <u>digging</u> in the mud.

8. The father <u>was</u> <u>talking</u> to the mother.

**To Do Activity**   Have the child tell about things he likes to do outside.   Have him draw pictures of himself doing these things.   Then, have him tell you what he was doing in each picture he drew.

# Worksheet 6A:  At the Park

Name _____

Use this scene with the scene on the next page.

Use this scene with the scene on the previous page.

## Worksheets 6A and 6B:  At the Park

**Posttest Directions**

Look at these two pictures.  The first picture shows people doing things.  In the second picture, they are finished doing these things.  Tell me what each person was doing.  (If the child has difficulty, provide a question prompt.  For example, point to the man painting and say,) Here, the man is painting.  (Then, point to the man in the next picture and say,) Now, he is done.  What was he doing?  (The child responds, *The man was painting.*  Continue until the child uses the past progressive in sentences such as:)

1.  The baby <u>was</u> <u>sleeping</u> on the blanket.

2.  The girl <u>was</u> <u>running</u> in the park.

3.  The people <u>were</u> <u>eating</u> at the picnic table.

4.  The children <u>were</u> <u>playing</u> jumprope on the grass.

5.  The old man <u>was</u> <u>sitting</u> on the park bench.

6.  The people <u>were</u> <u>walking</u> beside the pond.

7.  The artist <u>was</u> <u>painting</u> a picture.

8.  The girl <u>was</u> <u>crying</u> beside the man.

**To Do Activity**   Have the child color the people in the picture.  Then, have her make up a story, telling what each person was doing in the picture.

## Worksheet 1A:  Football Game

Use this scene with the scene on the next page.

Past Regular

47

# Worksheet 1B: Football Game

Use this scene with the scene on the previous page.

# Worksheets 1A and 1B:  Football Game

**Pretest Directions:  Expressive**

Look at these two pictures.  The first picture shows people and an animal doing things.  In the second picture, they are finished doing these things.  Tell me about each person and animal and what happened.  (Point to Worksheet 1B.  If the child has difficulty, provide a question prompt. For example, point to the cheerleaders jumping and say,)  Here, the girls are jumping.  (Then, point to the girls in the next picture and say,)  Now, they're done.  What did they do?  (The child responds, *The girls jumped.*  Continue until the child uses the past regular in sentences such as:)

1.  The cheerleaders jumped.

2.  The girl waved.

3.  The boy laughed.

4.  The football player kicked.

5.  The dog barked.

6.  The coach talked.

7.  The girl smiled.

8.  The man clapped.

**Pretest Directions:  Receptive**

Materials:  red, green, yellow, blue, purple, orange, black, and pink crayons

Let's practice listening carefully.  Look at these worksheets.  I will talk about what each person and animal did.  I will also tell you what to do on your worksheets.  (Present items randomly from both worksheets.)

1.  Listen.  Draw a red line under the ones who are jumping/jumped.

2.  Listen.  Draw a green line under the one who is waving/waved.

3.  Listen.  Draw a yellow line under the one who is laughing/laughed.

4.  Listen.  Draw a blue line under the one who is kicking/kicked.

5.  Listen.  Draw a purple line under the one that is barking/barked.

6.  Listen.  Draw an orange line under the one who is talking/talked.

7.  Listen.  Draw a black line under the one who is smiling/smiled.

8.  Listen.  Draw a pink line under the one who is clapping/clapped.

Good listening!

**Auditory Bombardment** Listen carefully. (Describe the actions, stressing the verb as you point to each picture.)
 The girl is jumping. Now, she's done.
  The girl jumped.
 The baby is waving. Now, he's done.
  The baby waved.

**Auditory Discrimination** Listen to what I say. Then, point to the picture I talk about. (Describe the pictures at random.)
 The girl is jumping.
 The girl jumped.
 The baby is waving.
 The baby waved.

**To Do Activity** Have the child color the pictures. Cut the pictures apart and paste them on four empty soup cans. Place the cans a short distance from the child and have him toss buttons into the cans with the pictures you describe.

Name _____

**Auditory Bombardment**   Listen carefully.
(Describe the actions, stressing the verb as you
point to each picture.)
    The clown is laughing.   Now, he's done.
        The clown laughed.
    The boy is kicking.   Now, he's done.
        The boy kicked.

**Auditory Discrimination**   Listen to what I say.
Then, point to the picture I talk about.   (Describe
the pictures at random.)
    The clown is laughing.
    The clown laughed.
    The boy is kicking.
    The boy kicked.

**To Do Activity**   Cut the pictures apart and mount them on brightly colored pieces of paper.   Place a small
metal paper clip under each picture.   Give the child a magnet and have her use it to pick up the pictures
you describe.

PAST REGULAR                                          51

Name _____

**Auditory Bombardment**   Listen carefully.
(Describe the actions, stressing the verb as you
point to each picture.)
    The dog is barking.   Now, it's done.
      The dog barked.
    The lady is talking.   Now, she's done.
      The lady talked.

**Auditory Discrimination**   Listen to what I say.
Then, point to the picture I talk about.   (Describe
the pictures at random.)
    The dog is barking.
    The dog barked.
    The lady is talking.
    The lady talked.

**To Do Activity**   Cut the pictures apart and mount them on pieces of red construction paper.   Describe the
pictures at random.   Let the child put the pieces of the hearts together if he identifies the pictures correctly.

52

**Auditory Bombardment**   Listen carefully.
(Describe the actions, stressing the verb as you point to each picture.)

    The man is smiling.   Now, he's done.
      The man smiled.
    The woman is clapping.   Now, she's done.
      The woman clapped.

**Auditory Discrimination**   Listen to what I say.
Then, point to the picture I talk about.   (Describe the pictures at random.)

    The man is smiling.
    The man smiled.
    The woman is clapping.
    The woman clapped.

**To Do Activity**   Have the child act out each picture with a hand puppet as you describe it.   For variety, have her act out the same pictures with different puppets.

PAST REGULAR                                    53

**Sentence Repetition**   (Point to each picture as you say:)

Listen.   The cheerleaders are jumping.   Now, they're done.   Say what I say:   The cheerleaders jumped.

Listen.   The girl is waving.   Now, she's done. Say what I say:   The girl waved.

**Sentence Production**   (Point to each picture and ask,) What is/are the ___ doing? (or) What did the ___ do?   (The child responds with sentences such as:)

The cheerleaders <u>are</u> <u>jumping</u>.
The cheerleaders <u>jumped</u>.
The girl <u>is</u> <u>waving</u>.
The girl <u>waved</u>.

**To Do Activity**   Cut the pictures apart.   Squeeze glue onto the frames around the pictures and have the child sprinkle glitter onto the glue if he describes the picture using a correct sentence.   Then, tap off the extra glitter.

54

**Sentence Repetition**  (Point to each picture as you say:)

    Listen.  The boy is laughing.  Now, he's done.  Say what I say:  The boy laughed.

    Listen.  The football player is kicking.  Now, he's done.  Say what I say:  The football player kicked.

**Sentence Production**  (Point to each picture and ask,) What is the ___ doing? (or) What did the ___ do?  (The child responds with sentences such as:)

    The boy is <u>laughing</u>.
    The boy <u>laughed</u>.
    The football player <u>is kicking</u>.
    The football player <u>kicked</u>.

**To Do Activity**  Have the child color the pictures.  Cut the pictures out and paste them onto four pieces of paper.  Have the child draw a design on a blank piece of paper of the same size.  Then, staple all the papers together like a booklet, with the design page on top and the pictures in correct time order.  Ask the child to ''read'' the story by describing the sequence of events.

**Sentence Repetition**   (Point to each picture as you say:)
    Listen.   The dog is barking.   Now, it's done.
      Say what I say:   The dog barked.
    Listen.   The coach is talking.   Now, he's done.
      Say what I say:   The coach talked.

**Sentence Production**   (Point to each picture and ask,) What is the ____ doing? (or) What did the ____ do?   (The child responds with sentences such as:)
    The dog is barking.
    The dog barked.
    The coach is talking.
    The coach talked.

**To Do Activity**   Cut these pictures apart and give the child a large piece of construction paper.   Have her pick a picture and glue it on the paper if she describes it using a correct sentence.   When she is finished, let her draw a background scene around the flowers (e.g., add stems, leaves, grass, etc.).

Name _____

**Sentence Repetition**   (Point to each picture as you say:)
    Listen.   The girl is smiling.   Now, she's done.
      Say what I say:   The girl smiled.
    Listen.   The man is clapping.   Now, he's done.
      Say what I say:   The man clapped.

**Sentence Production**   (Point to each picture and ask,) What is the ____ doing? (or) What did the ____ do?   (The child responds with sentences such as:)
    The girl is smiling.
    The girl smiled.
    The man is clapping.
    The man clapped.

**To Do Activity**   Have the child outline the "before" pictures, and color the "after" pictures.   Then, have him describe both sequences of events.

57

**Expanded Sentence Repetition** (Point to each picture as you say:)

　Listen.  The clown is jumping in the air.  Now, he's done.  Say what I say:  The clown jumped in the air.

　Listen.  The girl is waving at the crowd.  Now, she's done.  Say what I say:  The girl waved at the crowd.

**Expanded Sentence Production** (Point to each picture and ask,) What is the ___ doing? (or) What did the ___ do?  (The child responds with expanded sentences such as:)

　The clown is jumping in the air.
　The clown jumped in the air.
　The girl is waving at the crowd.
　The girl waved at the crowd.

**To Do Activity**　Play Simon Says with the child, taking turns being the leader.  Use the actions on these pictures as some of your commands.  Then, have the child tell you what she did.

**Expanded Sentence Repetition** (Point to each picture as you say:)

Listen. The girl is laughing at the clown. Now, she's done. Say what I say: The girl laughed at the clown.

Listen. The little boy is kicking the ball. Now, he's done. Say what I say: The little boy kicked the ball.

**Expanded Sentence Production** (Point to each picture and ask,) What is the ____ doing? (or) What did the ____ do? (The child responds with expanded sentences such as:)

The girl is laughing at the clown.
The girl laughed at the clown.
The little boy is kicking the ball.
The little boy kicked the ball.

**To Do Activity** Cut these pictures apart and give the child a large piece of construction paper. Have the child paste each picture on the paper. Let him draw candles to complete each cake if he describes the picture using a correct expanded sentence.

**Expanded Sentence Repetition**  (Point to each picture as you say:)

    Listen.  The dog is barking at the clown.  Now, it's done.  Say what I say:  The dog barked at the clown.

    Listen.  The little girl is talking to her doll.  Now, she's done.  Say what I say:  The little girl talked to her doll.

**Expanded Sentence Production**  (Point to each picture and ask,)  What is the ___ doing? (or) What did the ___ do?  (The child responds with expanded sentences such as:)

    The dog is barking at the clown.
    The dog barked at the clown.
    The little girl is talking to her doll.
    The little girl talked to her doll.

**To Do Activity**  Punch holes around the perimeter of the page.  Then, have the child string a piece of yarn or ribbon all the way around to frame the pictures.  Have her describe each of the pictures using a correct expanded sentence.

**Expanded Sentence Repetition**   (Point to each picture as you say:)
   Listen.   The lady is smiling at the little girl.
      Now, she's done.   Say what I say:   The lady smiled at the little girl.
   Listen.   The boy is clapping for the parade.
      Now, he's done.   Say what I say:   The boy clapped for the parade.

**Expanded Sentence Production**   (Point to each picture and ask,)  What is the ____ doing? (or) What did the ____ do?   (The child responds with sentences such as:)
   The lady is smiling at the little girl.
   The lady smiled at the little girl.
   The boy is clapping for the parade.
   The boy clapped for the parade.

**To Do Activity**   Give the child several watercolors and a brush.   Have him outline the people and animals in the pictures.   Then, have him describe the actions and the colors using correct expanded sentences.

## Worksheet 5A:   At the Parade

Use this scene with the scene on the next page.

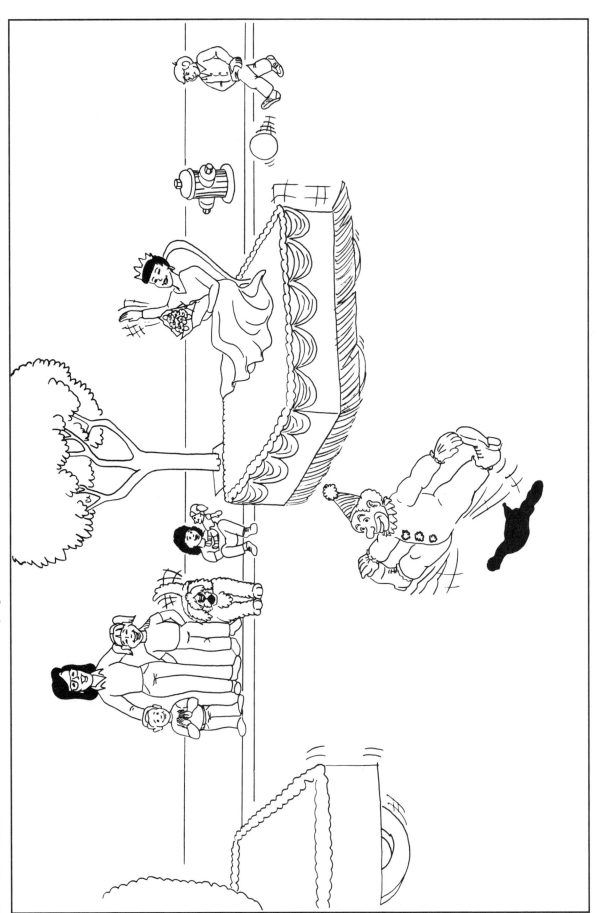

62

## Worksheet 5B:  At the Parade

Use this scene with the scene on the previous page.

# Worksheets 5A and 5B:   At the Parade

## Carryover Directions

Look at these two pictures.   The first picture shows people and an animal doing things.   In the second picture, they are finished doing these things.   Tell me all the things that happened in this picture.   (Point to Worksheet 5B.   If the child has difficulty, provide a question prompt.   For example, point to the girl who is waving and say,) Here, the girl is waving to the crowd.   (Then, point to the girl in the next picture and say,) Now, she is finished waving.   What did she do?   (The child responds, *The girl waved at the crowd.*   Continue until the child uses the past regular in sentences such as:)

1.   The girl waved to the crowd.

2.   The boy clapped his hands.

3.   The woman beside the boy smiled.

4.   The clown jumped in the air.

5.   The girl laughed at the clown.

6.   The dog barked at the clown.

7.   The girl talked to her doll.

8.   The boy kicked a ball.


**To Do Activity**   Have the child press her finger lightly onto an ink pad.   Then, have her press her finger on each action in the pictures as she describes it.

Name _____

## Worksheet 6A: At the Basketball Game

Use this scene with the scene on the next page.

## Worksheet 6B:  At the Basketball Game

Use this scene with the scene on the previous page.

# Worksheets 6A and 6B:   Basketball Game   Name _____

## Posttest Directions

Look at these two pictures.   The first picture shows people doing things.   In the second picture, they are finished doing these things.   Tell me all the things that happened in this picture.   (Point to Worksheet 6B.   If the child has difficulty, provide a question prompt.   For example, point to the girl bouncing the ball and say,) Here, the girl is bouncing the ball.   (Then, point to the girl in the next picture and say,) Now, she's done.   What did she do?   (The child responds, *The girl bounced the ball.*   Continue until the child uses the past regular in sentences such as:)

1.   The girl <u>bounced</u> the ball.

2.   The boy <u>walked</u> to his seat.

3.   The lady <u>watched</u> the game.

4.   The child <u>dropped</u> his popcorn.

5.   The man <u>combed</u> his hair.

6.   The coach <u>yelled</u> to her team.

7.   The cheerleaders <u>cheered</u> for the players.

8.   The band <u>played</u> a song.

**To Do Activity**   Paste the pictures onto a piece of cardboard.   Then, have the child decorate each picture with small pieces of colored felt and little beads.   When he's finished, have him use sentences to talk about the different actions in the pictures.

## Worksheet 1A:  At the Baseball Game

Use this scene with the scene on the next page.

69

Past Irregular

**Worksheet 1B:  At the Baseball Game**

Use this scene with the scene on the previous page.

70

## Worksheets 1A and 1B:   At the Baseball Game

### Pretest Directions:   Expressive

Look at these two pictures.   The first picture shows people and an animal doing things.   In the second picture, they are finished doing these things.   Tell me about each person and animal and what happened.   (Point to Worksheet 1B.   If the child has difficulty, use a question prompt.   For example, point to the boy selling popcorn and say,) Here, the boy is standing.   (Then, point to the same boy in the next picture and say,) Now, he isn't.   What did he do?   (The child answers, *The boy stood*.   Continue until the child uses the past irregular in sentences such as:)

1.   The boy stood.

2.   The man ate.

3.   The runner slid.

4.   The bat boy drank.

5.   The bird flew.

6.   The girl sat.

7.   The player ran.

8.   The baby slept.

### Pretest Directions:   Receptive

Materials:   red, green, yellow, blue, purple, orange, black, and pink crayons

Let's practice listening carefully.   Look at your worksheets.   I will talk about what each person and animal did.   I will also tell you what to do on your worksheets.   (Present items randomly from both worksheets.)

1.   Listen.   Draw a red line around the one who is standing/stood.

2.   Listen.   Draw a green line around the one who is eating/ate.

3.   Listen.   Draw a yellow line around the one who is sliding/slid.

4.   Listen.   Draw a blue line around the one who is drinking/drank.

5.   Listen.   Draw a purple line around the one that is flying/flew.

6.   Listen.   Draw an orange line around the one who is sitting/sat.

7.   Listen.   Draw a black line around the one who is running/ran.

8.   Listen.   Draw a pink line around the one who is sleeping/slept.

Good listening!

71

Name _____

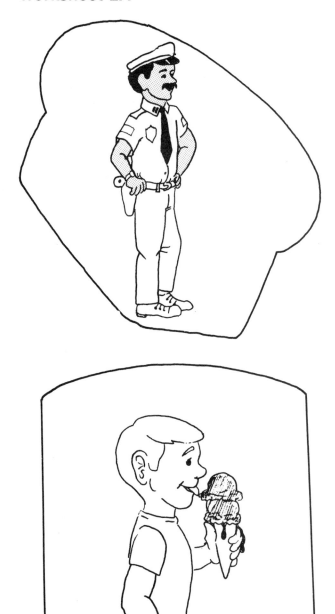

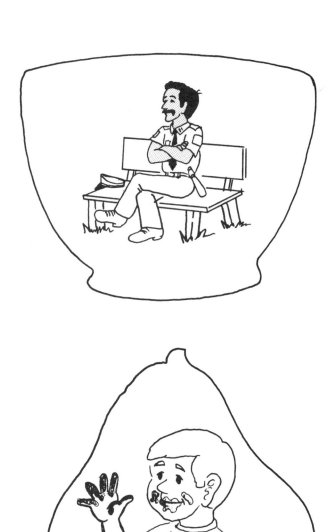

**Auditory Bombardment**   Listen carefully. (Describe the actions, stressing the past irregular verbs as you point to each picture.)
    The police officer is standing.   Now, he isn't.
      The police officer stood.
    The boy is eating.   Now, he's done.
      The boy ate.

**Auditory Discrimination**   Listen to what I say. Then, point to the picture I talk about.   (Describe the pictures at random.)
    The police officer is standing.
    The police officer stood.
    The boy is eating.
    The boy ate.

**To Do Activity**   Have the child cut out these pictures and paste them on small paper plates.   Then, have the child put the pictures in the correct sequence as you describe them.

72

**Auditory Bombardment**   Listen carefully.
(Describe the actions, stressing the past irregular
verbs as you point to each picture.)
    The girl is sliding.   Now, she's done.
      The girl slid.
    The nurse is drinking.   Now, she's done.
      The nurse drank.

**Auditory Discrimination**   Listen to what I say.
Then, point to the picture I talk about.   (Describe
the pictures at random.)
    The girl is sliding.
    The girl slid.
    The nurse is drinking.
    The nurse drank.

**To Do Activity**   Have the child glue uncooked spaghetti pieces on the pictures, framing the people as you
describe the actions.

**Auditory Bombardment**   Listen carefully.
(Describe the actions, stressing the past irregular
verbs as you point to each picture.)
   The airplane is flying.   Now, it isn't.   The
     airplane flew.
   The coach is sitting.   Now, she isn't.   The
     coach sat.

**Auditory Discrimination**   Listen to what I say.
Then, point to the picture I talk about.   (Describe
the pictures at random.)
   The airplane is flying.
   The airplane flew.
   The coach is sitting.
   The coach sat.

**To Do Activity**   Have the child act out each picture.   Describe what she is doing.   When she's done, tell
her what she did.

Name _____

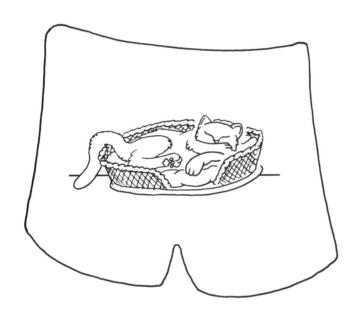

**Auditory Bombardment**   Listen carefully.
(Describe the actions, stressing the past irregular
verbs as you point to each picture.)
　　The lady is running.   Now, she's done.
　　　The lady ran.
　　The cat is sleeping.   Now, it's done.
　　　The cat slept.

**Auditory Discrimination**   Listen to what I say.
Then, point to the picture I talk about.   (Describe
the pictures at random.)
　　The lady is running.
　　The lady ran.
　　The cat is sleeping.
　　The cat slept.

**To Do Activity**   Have the child color each picture.   Next, cut each picture out and paste it on a piece of
construction paper.   Then, have the child put the pictures in the correct sequence and attach them to a
"clothesline" (a piece of string or rope) with clothespins or paper clips as you describe them.

75

**Sentence Repetition**  (Point to each picture as you say:)
   Listen.   The boy is standing.   Now, he isn't.
      Say what I say:   The boy stood.
   Listen.   The man is eating.   Now, he's done.
      Say what I say:   The man ate.

**Sentence Production**  (Point to each picture and ask,) What is the ___ doing? (or) What did the ___ do? (The child responds with sentences such as:)
   The boy is standing.
   The boy stood.
   The man is eating.
   The man ate.

**To Do Activity**   Cut the pictures out and paste them on a block or paper cube.   Have the child toss the block into the air.   When it lands, have him use a correct sentence to describe the picture that is shown on top.

**Sentence Repetition** (Point to each picture as you say:)

Listen.   The runner is sliding.   Now, he's done.
Say what I say:   The runner slid.
Listen.   The bat boy is drinking.   Now, he's
done.   Say what I say:   The bat boy drank.

**Sentence Production**   (Point to each picture and ask,) What is the ___ doing? (or) What did the ___ do?   (The child responds with sentences such as:)

The runner is sliding.
The runner slid.
The bat boy is drinking.
The bat boy drank.

**To Do Activity**   Cut the pictures apart like four jigsaw puzzle pieces.   Have the child glue the pieces back together on a piece of cardboard if she describes the pictures using correct sentences.

**Sentence Repetition**   (Point to each picture as you say:)
   Listen.   The bird is flying.   Now, it's done.
      Say what I say:   The bird flew.
   Listen.   The girl is standing.   Now, she isn't.
      Say what I say:   The girl stood.

**Sentence Production**   (Point to each picture and ask,) What is the ____ doing? (or) What did the ____ do?   (The child responds with sentences such as:)
   The bird is flying.
   The bird flew.
   The girl is standing.
   The girl stood.

**To Do Activity**   Have the child color each picture.   Decorate a shoe box to look like a flower box with stems and leaves coming out of the dirt.   Cut the pictures apart and let the child paste them on the stems in the correct sequence if he describes the actions using correct sentences.

78

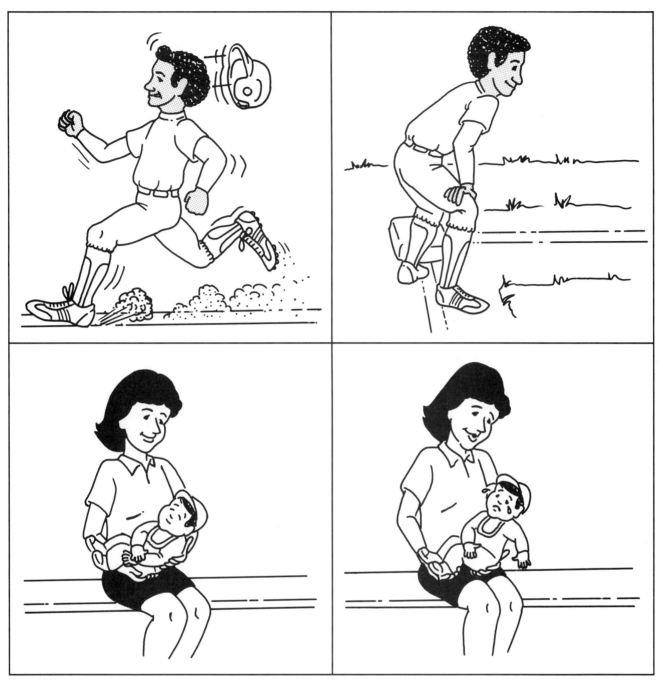

**Sentence Repetition**  (Point to each picture as you say:)
    Listen.  The player is running.  Now, he's done.
      Say what I say:  The player ran.
    Listen.  The baby is sleeping.  Now, he's done.
      Say what I say:  The baby slept.

**Sentence Production**  (Point to each picture and ask,)  What is the ___ doing? (or)  What did the ___ do?  (The child responds with sentences such as:)
    The player is running.
    The player ran.
    The baby is sleeping.
    The baby slept.

**To Do Activity**  Have the child color the pictures and cut them out.  Cut out additional strips of plain white paper.  Then, have the child paste the pictures together to make a paper chain and hang them in the room. Have the child describe the different actions in the paper chain using correct sentences.

Name _____

**Expanded Sentence Repetition**   (Point to each picture as you say:)

　　Listen.   The man is standing near his son.
　　　Now, he isn't.   Say what I say:   The man
　　　stood near his son.
　　Listen.   The boy is eating a candy bar.   Now,
　　　he's done.   Say what I say:   The boy ate
　　　a candy bar.

**Expanded Sentence Production**   (Point to each picture and ask,) What is the ___ doing? (or) What did the ___ do?   (The child responds with expanded sentences such as:)

　　The man <u>is standing</u> near his son.
　　The man <u>stood</u> near his son.
　　The boy <u>is eating</u> a candy bar.
　　The boy <u>ate</u> a candy bar.

**To Do Activity**   Cut the pictures apart and mount them on pieces of construction paper.   Have the child look away while you remove one of the pictures.   Then, ask her to recall the missing picture and describe it using a correct expanded sentence.

80

**Expanded Sentence Repetition**  (Point to each picture as you say:)

    Listen.   The girl is sliding down the hill.   Now, she's done.   Say what I say:   The girl slid down the hill.

    Listen.   The man is drinking hot chocolate. Now, he's done.   Say what I say:   The man drank hot chocolate.

**Expanded Sentence Production**  (Point to each picture and ask,)  What is the ___ doing? (or) What did the ___ do?  (The child responds with expanded sentences such as:)

    The girl <u>is</u> <u>sliding</u> down the hill.
    The girl <u>slid</u> down the hill.
    The man <u>is</u> <u>drinking</u> hot chocolate.
    The man <u>drank</u> hot chocolate.

**To Do Activity**   Have the child cut small pieces of colored yarn.   Have him glue the yarn on the pictures, outlining the objects and people.   Then, ask him to describe the pictures using correct expanded sentences.

81

**Expanded Sentence Repetition**　(Point to each picture as you say:)

   Listen.　The airplane is flying by.　Now, it isn't.
   Say what I say:　The airplane flew by.
   Listen.　The lady is sitting on the bench.　Now, she isn't.　Say what I say:　The lady sat on the bench.

**Expanded Sentence Production**　(Point to each picture and ask,)　What is the ___ doing? (or) What did the ___ do?　(The child responds with expanded sentences such as:)

   The airplane <u>is flying</u> by.
   The airplane <u>flew</u> by.
   The lady <u>is sitting</u> on the bench.
   The lady <u>sat</u> on the bench.

**To Do Activity**　Have the child color the pictures.　Then, cut the pictures apart and paste them on Styrofoam or paper cups.　Have the child arrange the cups in the correct sequence and describe the actions using correct expanded sentences.

　　　　82

**Expanded Sentence Repetition**  (Point to each picture as you say:)

    Listen.  The girl is running to her mom.  Now, she isn't.  Say what I say:  The girl ran to her mom.

    Listen.  The dog is sleeping by the tree.  Now, he isn't.  Say what I say:  The dog slept by the tree.

**Expanded Sentence Production**  (Point to each picture and ask,) What is the ___ doing? (or) What did the ___ do?  (The child responds with expanded sentences such as:)

    The girl is running to her mom.
    The girl ran to her mom.
    The dog is sleeping by the tree.
    The dog slept by the tree.

**To Do Activity**  Cut the pictures apart.  Have the child paste the pictures that go together on two long strips of paper with extra space between them.  Next, have the child draw a picture of what could happen between each of the pictures.  Then, have her describe the new sequence of events using correct expanded sentences.

83

## Worksheet 5A:  A Snowy Day

Use this scene with the scene on the next page.

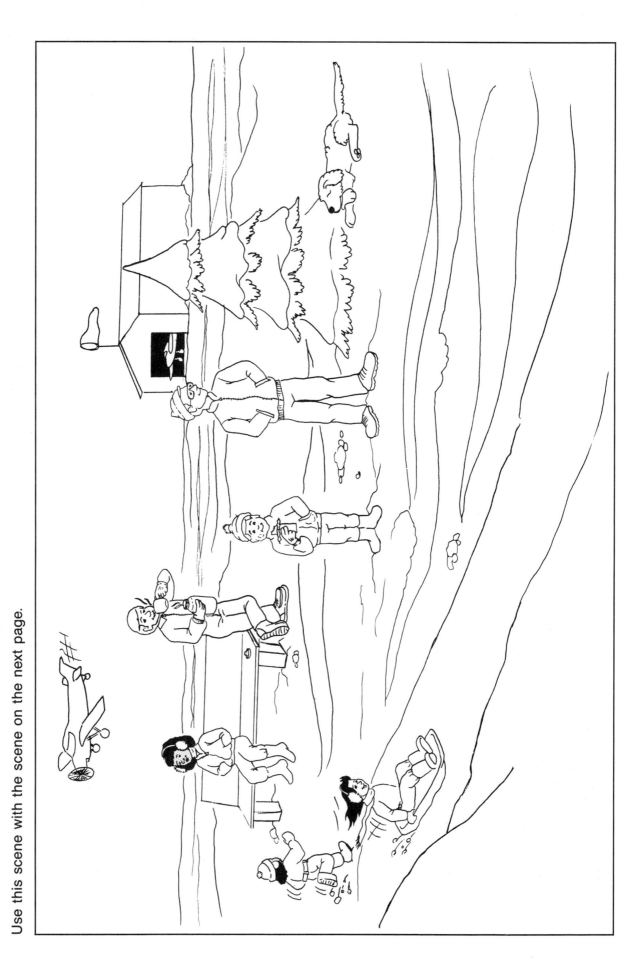

# Worksheet 5B: A Snowy Day

Use this scene with the scene on the previous page.

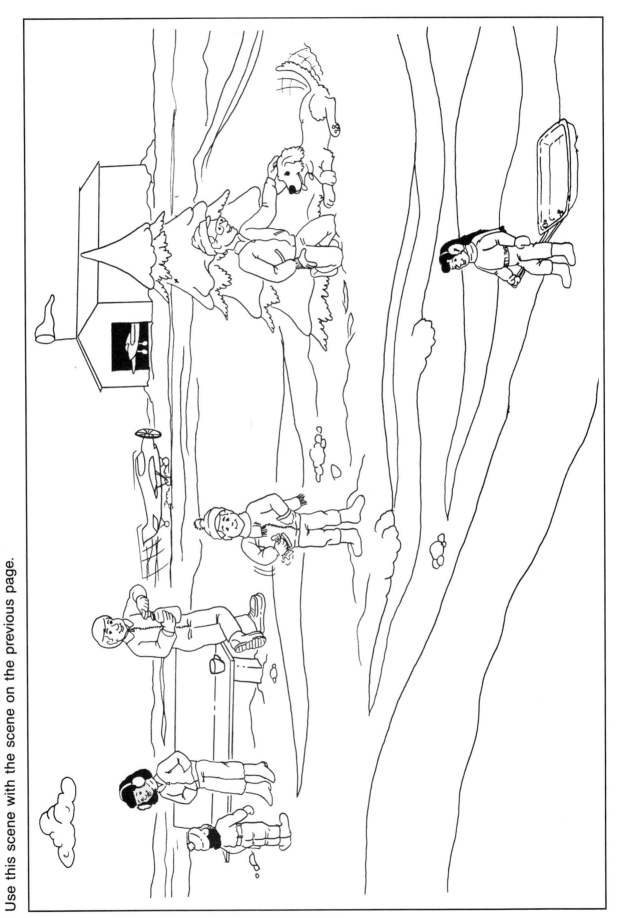

## Worksheets 5A and 5B:   A Snowy Day

### Carryover Directions

Look at these two pictures.   The first picture shows people and things in action.   In the second picture, this action is finished.   Tell me all the things that happened in this picture.   (Point to Worksheet 5B.   If the child has difficulty, provide a question prompt.   For example, point to the dad and say,) Here, Dad is standing near his son.   (Then, point to the dad in the next picture and say,) Now, he isn't.   What did he do?   (The child answers, *Dad* <u>stood</u> *near his son.*   Continue until the child uses the irregular past in sentences such as:)

1.   Dad <u>stood</u> near his son.

2.   The boy <u>ate</u> a candy bar.

3.   The girl <u>slid</u> down the hill.

4.   The man <u>drank</u> hot chocolate.

5.   The airplane <u>flew</u> above their heads.

6.   The lady <u>sat</u> on the bench.

7.   The girl <u>ran</u> to her mom.

8.   The dog <u>slept</u> by the tree.

**To Do Activity**   Have the child tell you a story about the pictures using correct past tense sentences.   Write down the main points and put them in paragraph form on a piece of paper. Have the child color the different actions in the pictures as you read the story back to him.   Let him take his story home and have his parents read it aloud.

## Worksheet 6A:  At the Swimming Pool

Use this scene with the scene on the next page.

87

## Worksheet 6B: At the Swimming Pool

Use this scene with the scene on the previous page.

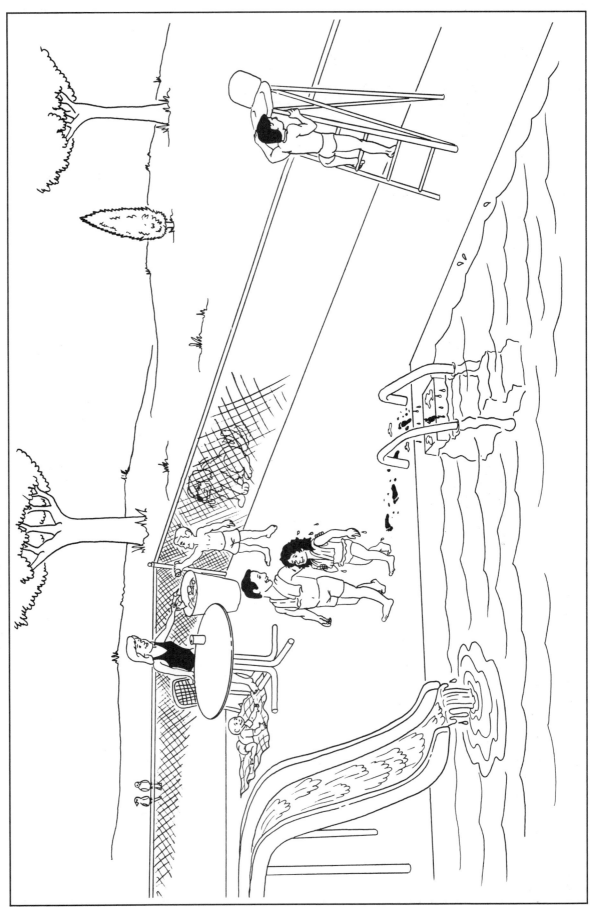

88

# Worksheets 6A and 6B:
# At the Swimming Pool

Name _____

## Posttest Directions

Look at these two pictures.   The first picture shows people and animals doing things.   In the second picture, they are finished doing these things.   Tell me all the things that happened in this picture.   (Point to Worksheet 6B.   If the child has difficulty, provide a question prompt.   For example, point to the lady eating a hot dog and say,) Here, the lady is eating a hot dog.   (Then, point to the lady in the next picture and say,) Now, she is finished.   What did she do?   (The child answers, *The lady ate a hot dog.*   Continue until the child uses the past irregular in sentences such as:)

1.   The lady ate a hot dog.

2.   The man stood by the slide.

3.   The birds flew by.

4.   The baby slept on a quilt.

5.   The girl slid down the slide.

6.   The lifeguard sat in his chair.

7.   The dog ran outside the fence.

8.   The boy drank soda pop.

**To Do Activity**   Have the child draw an X on every action in the pictures.   Then, have her use correct sentences and a hand puppet to tell what might have happened yesterday.

Name _____

**Worksheet 1:  At the Beach**

91

## Worksheet 1:  At the Beach

**Pretest Directions:  Expressive**

Look at this picture.  Tell me what each person does.  (If the child has difficulty, point to one of the people and say,)  Tell me what the ___ does.  (Continue until the child describes all the action with sentences such as:)

1.  The boy <u>drinks</u>.

2.  The man <u>drives</u>.

3.  The boy <u>swims</u>.

4.  The girl <u>draws</u>.

5.  The boy <u>listens</u>.

6.  The girl <u>dances</u>.

7.  The woman <u>reads</u>.

8.  The man <u>sneezes</u>.

**Pretest Directions:  Receptive**

Materials:  blue, red, green, purple, yellow, orange, pink, and black crayons

Let's practice listening carefully.  Look at your worksheet.  There are many people doing things. I will talk about each person and tell you what to do on your worksheet.

1.  Listen.  Draw a blue line under the person who drinks.

2.  Listen.  Draw a red line under the person who drives.

3.  Listen.  Draw a green line under the person who swims.

4.  Listen.  Draw a purple line under the person who draws.

5.  Listen.  Draw a yellow line under the person who listens.

6.  Listen.  Draw an orange line under the person who dances.

7.  Listen.  Draw a pink line under the person who reads.

8.  Listen.  Draw a black line under the person who sneezes.

Nice work!

Name _____

**Auditory Bombardment**   Listen carefully.
(Describe the actions, stressing the verbs as you
slowly point to each picture.)
   The girl drinks.
   The woman drives.
   The swan swims.
   The girl draws.

**Auditory Discrimination**   Listen to what I say.
Then, point to the picture I talk about.   (Ask about
the pictures at random.)
   Show me . . . who drinks.
                     who drives.
                     what swims.
                     who draws.

**To Do Activity**   Cut these pictures apart and give the child a piece of construction paper, some paste, and
a crayon.   Have the child point to the picture you describe.   If she is correct, let her paste that wing of
the butterfly on the paper.   When she has two wings that go together, let her draw in the body section and
color the pictures to complete the butterfly.

93

**Auditory Bombardment**   Listen carefully.
(Describe the actions, stressing the verbs as you slowly point to each picture.)
- The boy listens.
- The woman dances.
- The woman reads.
- The boy sneezes.

**Auditory Discrimination**   Listen to what I say.
Then, point to the picture I talk about.   (Ask about the pictures at random.)
- Show me who . . . listens.
- dances.
- reads.
- sneezes.

**To Do Activity**   Cut these pictures apart and mount them on colored poster board.   Lay the pictures on the table in front of the child and play charades.   Take turns acting out one of the pictures and having the other person guess which picture.   Describe the picture for the child as it is identified.

Name _____

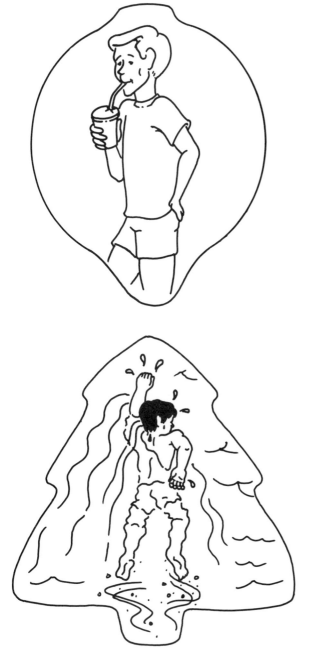

**Sentence Repetition**   Say what I say.   (Point to each picture as you say:)
   The boy drinks.
   The man drives.
   The boy swims.
   The girl draws.

**Sentence Production**   (Point to each picture and ask,) What does the ___ do?   (The child responds with sentences such as:)
   The boy <u>drinks</u>.
   The man <u>drives</u>.
   The boy <u>swims</u>.
   The girl <u>draws</u>.

**To Do Activity**   Cut these pictures apart and make an outline of a Christmas tree on poster board.   Have the child choose an ornament and paste it on the tree if he describes the picture correctly in a sentence. When he is finished, let him color the pictures.

THIRD PERSON SINGULAR                                      95

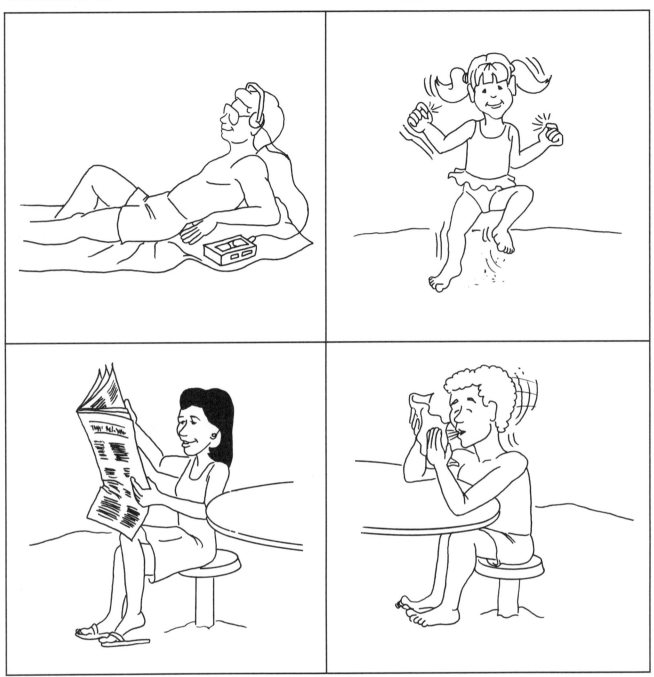

**Sentence Repetition**   Say what I say.   (Point to each picture as you say:)
> The boy listens.
> The girl dances.
> The woman reads.
> The man sneezes.

**Sentence Production**   (Point to each picture and ask,) What does the ___ do?   (The child responds with sentences such as:)
> The boy <u>listens</u>.
> The girl <u>dances</u>.
> The woman <u>reads</u>.
> The man <u>sneezes</u>.

**To Do Activity**   Cut these pictures apart and mount them on paper marked to correspond with a spinner (e.g., numbered from one to four to match the numbers, or on colored paper to match the colors of the spinner).   Have the child spin the spinner and use a correct sentence to describe the picture that corresponds with where the arrow lands.

Name _____

**Expanded Sentence Repetition**   Say what I say. (Point to each picture as you say:)
    The girl drinks a shake.
    The woman drives her car.
    The duck swims in the pond.
    The boy draws a picture.

**Expanded Sentence Production**   (Point to each picture and ask,) What does the _____ do?   (The child responds with expanded sentences such as:)
    The girl <u>drinks</u> a shake.
    The woman <u>drives</u> her car.
    The duck <u>swims</u> in the pond.
    The boy <u>draws</u> a picture.

**To Do Activity**   Cut these pictures apart and scatter them on the table.   Have the child close her eyes and point to one of the pictures.   If she uses a correct expanded sentence to describe the picture, she puts it in her pile.   See if she can collect all the pictures.

THIRD PERSON SINGULAR                                                          

**Expanded Sentence Repetition**   Say what I say.
(Point to each picture as you say:)
   The girl listens to her radio.
   The woman dances on stage.
   The man with glasses reads the program.
   The man sneezes loudly.

**Expanded Sentence Production**   (Point to each
picture and ask,) What does the ___ do?   (The
child responds with expanded sentences such as:)
   The girl <u>listens</u> to her radio.
   The woman <u>dances</u> on stage.
   The man with <u>glasses</u> <u>reads</u> the program.
   The man <u>sneezes</u> loudly.

**To Do Activity**   Cut these pictures apart and give the child a large piece of paper, some crayons, and paste.
Have the child choose a picture and describe it correctly in a sentence.   Next, let him paste the picture on
the piece of paper.   See if he can position all the pieces to make a scene.   Then, have him complete the
scene by drawing in other details, such as trees or chairs.

## Worksheet 5: At the Ballet

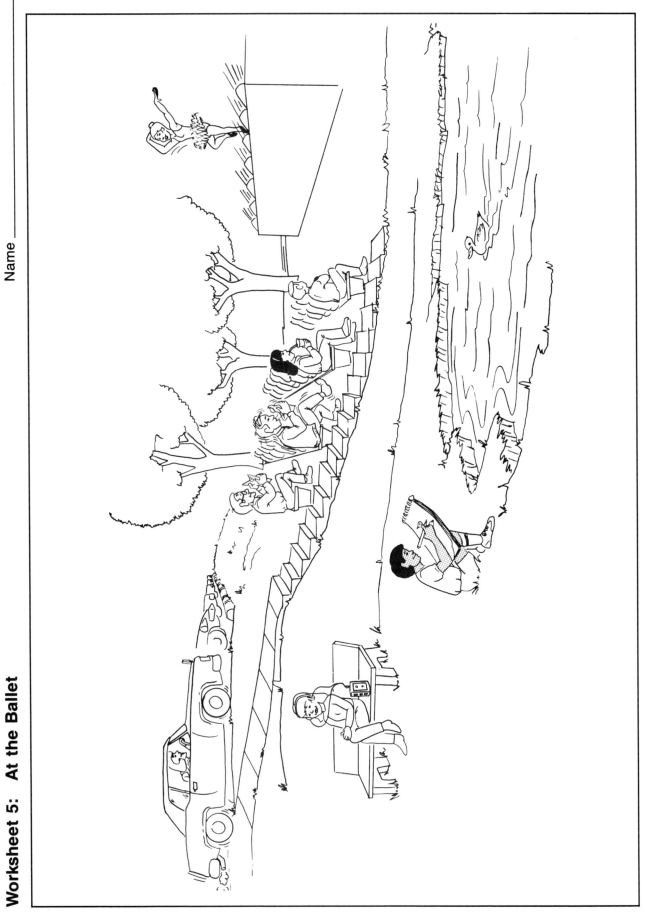

# Worksheet 5: At the Ballet

## Carryover Directions

Tell me about this picture. (If the child has difficulty, point to one of the action sequences and ask,) What does the ___ do? (Continue with the task until the child describes all the action with sentences such as:)

1. The girl <u>drinks</u> a shake.

2. The woman <u>drives</u> her car into the lot.

3. The duck <u>swims</u> in the pond.

4. The boy <u>draws</u> a picture.

5. The girl <u>listens</u> to her radio.

6. The woman <u>dances</u> on stage.

7. The man with glasses <u>reads</u> the program.

8. The old man <u>sneezes</u> loudly.

## To Do Activity

Make a verb booklet with the child. Cut out pictures from magazines of these same verbs and have the child paste them on the pages of the booklet, grouping the pictures according to the action. Then, take turns describing the action in each picture using expanded sentences.

**Worksheet 6:   Breakfast Time**

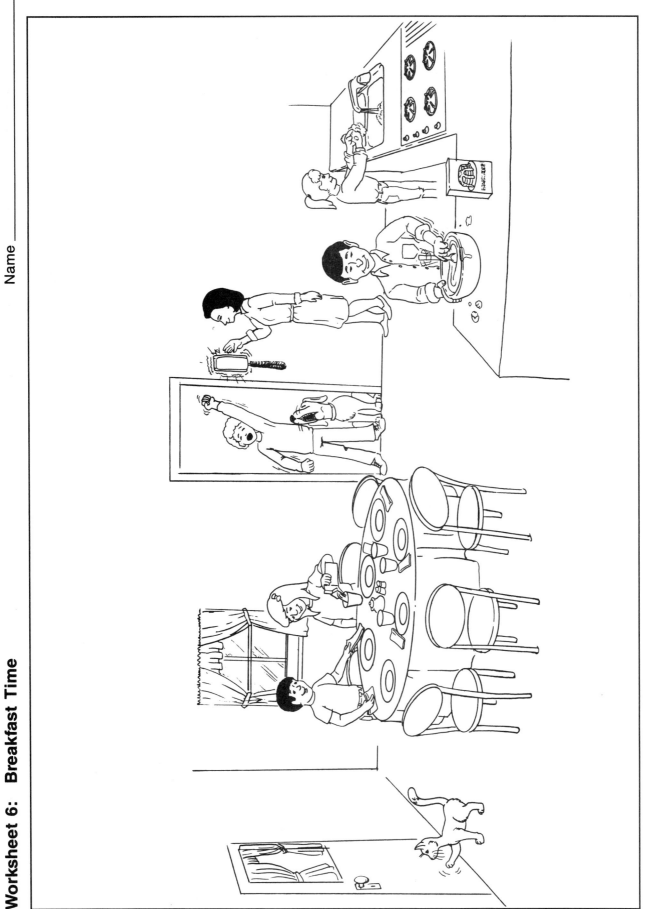

# Worksheet 6:   Breakfast Time

## Posttest Directions

Here are some pictures.   Tell me what each person and animal does.   Tell me all about them.
(If the child has difficulty, point to one of the action sequences and ask,) What does the ___ do?
(Continue until the child describes all the action with sentences such as:)

1.   The girl <u>washes</u> her hands.

2.   The father <u>fixes</u> pancakes in the kitchen.

3.   The boy <u>stretches</u> to wake up.

4.   The dog <u>yawns</u> at the boy's feet.

5.   The mother <u>answers</u> the phone.

6.   The boy <u>sets</u> the table.

7.   The cat <u>scratches</u> the door.

8.   The girl <u>pours</u> the milk into the glass.

## To Do Activity

Cut the individual action sequences out of this scene.   Have the child use a correct expanded
sentence to describe the action in each picture and predict what happens next, again using a
correct expanded sentence.   Let her draw a picture of the next action for each of these pictures
and paste the pictures in order on another sheet of paper.   When she is finished, have her take
her ''mini-stories'' home and tell them to her parents.

Name _____

Use this scene with the scene on the next page.

Future

103

Use this scene with the scene on the previous page.

# Worksheets 1A and 1B:  At the Park

## Pretest Directions:  Expressive

Look at these two pictures.  The first picture shows people doing things.  The second picture shows what they will do next.  Now, let's look at the first picture again.  Tell me what each person in this picture will do.  (Point to Worksheet 1A.  If the child has difficulty, provide a question prompt.  For example, point to the people sitting and say,)  Here, the people are sitting.  (Then, point to the people in the next picture, then back to the first picture, and ask,)  What will they do next?  (The child answers, *They will walk.*  Continue until the child uses the future in sentences such as:)

1.  The people will walk.

2.  The woman will run.

3.  The children will play.

4.  The baby will sleep.

5.  The people will eat.

6.  The girl will cry.

7.  The artist will paint.

8.  The man will sit.

## Pretest Directions:  Receptive

Materials:  red, green, yellow, blue, purple, orange, black, and pink crayons

Let's practice listening carefully.  Look at your worksheets.  There are many people doing things.  I will talk about each person and what will happen.  I will also tell you what to do on your worksheets.  (Present items randomly from both worksheets.)

1.  Listen.  Draw a red X on what I say.  The people will walk/are walking.

2.  Listen.  Draw a green X on what I say.  The woman will run/is running.

3.  Listen.  Draw a yellow X on what I say.  The children will play/are playing.

4.  Listen.  Draw a blue X on what I say.  The baby will sleep/is sleeping.

5.  Listen.  Draw a purple X on what I say.  The people will eat/are eating.

6.  Listen.  Draw an orange X on what I say.  The girl will cry/is crying.

7.  Listen.  Draw a black X on what I say.  The artist will paint/is painting.

8.  Listen.  Draw a pink X on what I say.  The man will sit/is sitting.

Good listening!

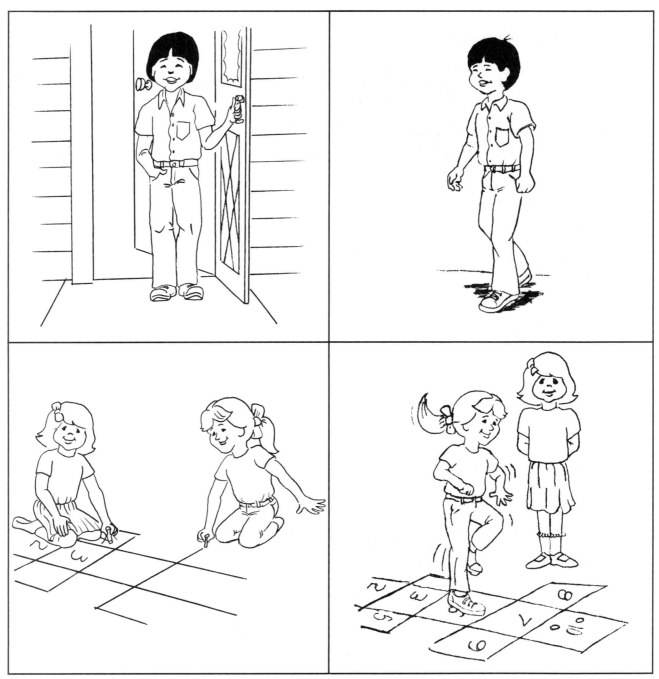

**Auditory Bombardment**  Listen carefully.
(Describe the actions as you slowly point to each
picture.)

    The boy is at the door.  (Point to the second
      picture, then back to the first picture and say,)
      What will he do next?  He will walk.
    The girls are drawing on the sidewalk.  (Point to
      the second picture, then back to the first
      picture and say,)  What will the girls do next?
      They will play.

**Auditory Discrimination**  Listen to what I say.
Then, point to the picture I talk about.  (Describe
the pictures at random.)

    The boy will walk.
    The boy is walking.
    The girls will play.
    The girls are playing.

**To Do Activity**  Make an action mobile.  First, have the child color each person.  Then, cut the pictures
apart, paste them on pieces of colored construction paper, and tie a piece of yarn to each one.  If the child
points to the picture you describe, help her tie it to a hanger to make the mobile.

**Auditory Bombardment**　Listen carefully.
(Describe the actions as you slowly point to each picture.)
　The dog is jumping.　(Point to the second
　　picture, then back to the first picture and say,)
　　What will it do next?　It will eat.
　The boy is putting on a paint shirt.　(Point to the
　　second picture, then back to the first picture
　　and say,)　What will he do next?　He will paint.

**Auditory Discrimination**　Listen to what I say.
Then, point to the picture I talk about.　(Describe
the pictures at random.)
　The dog will eat.
　The dog is eating.
　The boy will paint.
　The boy is painting.

**To Do Activity**　Cut these pictures apart and mount them on pieces of construction paper.　Have the child
choose a piece and add it to the train if he identifies the picture correctly.

**Auditory Bombardment**   Listen carefully.
(Describe the actions as you slowly point to each picture.)

    The girl is tying her shoes.   (Point to the second picture, then back to the first picture and say,) What will she do next?   She will run.

    The cat is jumping up.   (Point to the second picture, then back to the first picture and say,) What will it do next?   It will sleep.

**Auditory Discrimination**   Listen to what I say. Then, point to the picture I talk about.   (Describe the pictures at random.)

    The girl will run.
    The girl is running.
    The cat will sleep.
    The cat is sleeping.

**To Do Activity**   Have the child color the pictures.   Cut the pictures apart and paste them on four empty soup cans.   Place the cans a short distance from the child and have her toss buttons into the cans with the pictures you describe.

           **108**         

Name _____

**Auditory Bombardment**   Listen carefully. (Describe the actions as you slowly point to each picture.)

The babies are falling down.   (Point to the second picture, then back to the first picture and say,) What will they do next?   They will cry.

The people are tired.   (Point to the second picture, then back to the first picture and say,) What will they do next?   They will sit.

**Auditory Discrimination**   Listen to what I say. Then, point to the picture I talk about.   (Describe the pictures at random.)

The babies will cry.
The babies are crying.
The people will sit.
The people are sitting.

**To Do Activity**   Cut the pictures apart and mount them on brightly colored pieces of paper.   Place a small metal paper clip under each picture.   Give the child a magnet and have him use it to pick up the picture you describe.

109

**Sentence Repetition**  (Point to each picture as you say:)
  Listen.  The people are sitting.  What will they do next?  Say this:  They will walk.
  Listen.  The children are talking.  What will they do next?  Say this:  They will play.

**Sentence Production**  (Point to the first picture in each pair and say,) The people are sitting. (or) The children are playing.  What will they do next? (The child responds with sentences such as:)
  The people <u>will</u> <u>walk</u>.
  The children <u>will</u> <u>play</u>.

**To Do Activity**  Cut these pictures apart and mount them on pieces of construction paper.  Make a dog or use a stuffed dog to go with the bones.  Let the child pick a bone and give it to the dog if she describes the picture using a correct sentence.

110

**Sentence Repetition**  (Point to each picture as you say:)

    Listen.   The woman is tying her shoes.   What
      will she do next?   Say this:   She will run.
    Listen.   The baby is drinking.   What will she do
      next?   Say this:   She will sleep.

**Sentence Production**  (Point to the first picture in
each pair and say,) The woman is tying her shoes.
(or) The baby is drinking.   What will she do next?
(The child responds with sentences such as:)

    The woman will run.
    The baby will sleep.

**To Do Activity**   Have the child color the pictures.   Cut the pictures out and paste them on four pieces of
paper.   Have the child draw a design on a blank piece of paper of the same size.   Then, staple all the
papers together like a booklet, with the design page on top and the pictures in correct time order.   Ask the
child to "read" the story by describing the sequence of events in correct sentences.

111

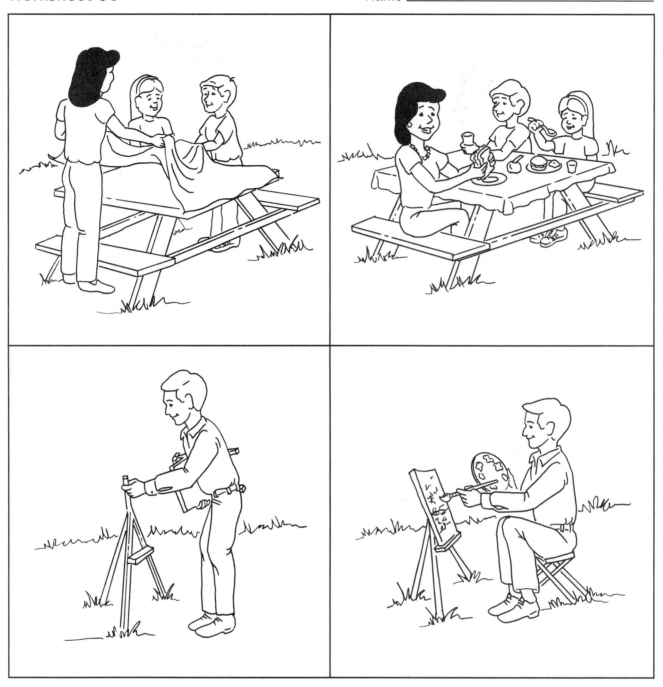

**Sentence Repetition**  (Point to each picture as you say:)

    Listen.  The people are spreading the tablecloth. What will they do next?  Say this:  They will eat.

    Listen.  The artist is putting up the easel.  What will he do next?  Say this:  He will paint.

**Sentence Production**  (Point to the first picture in each pair and say,) The people are spreading the tablecloth. (or) The artist is putting up the easel. What will they/he do next?  (The child responds with sentences such as:)

    The people <u>will</u> <u>eat</u>.

    The artist <u>will</u> <u>paint</u>.

**To Do Activity**  Place a piece of sandpaper under this page.  Have the child color each picture after he describes it correctly in a sentence.  The sandpaper will give the picture a textured look.

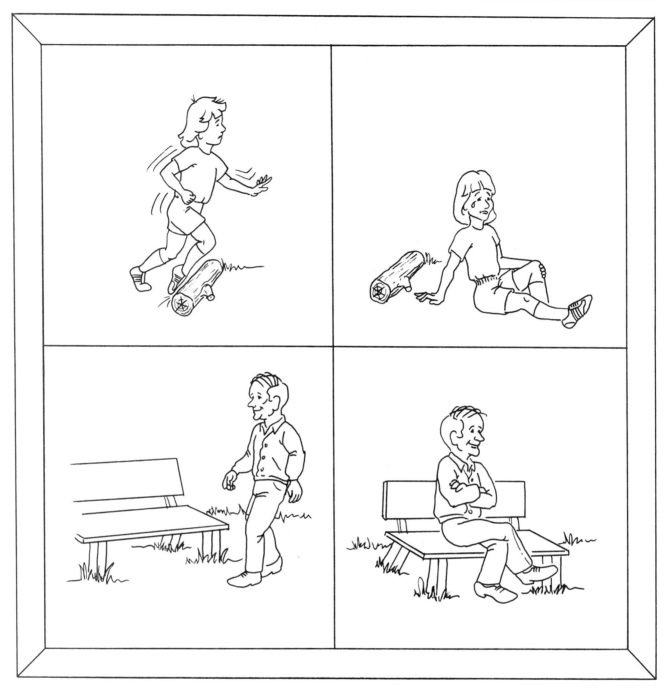

**Sentence Repetition**  (Point to each picture as you say:)

   Listen.   The girl is tripping over the log.   What will she do next?   Say this:   She will cry.

   Listen.   The man is walking to the bench.   What will he do next?   Say this:   He will sit.

**Sentence Production**   (Point to the first picture in each pair and say,) The girl is tripping. (or) The man is walking.   What will she/he do next?   (The child responds with sentences such as:)

   The girl <u>will</u> <u>cry</u>.
   The man <u>will</u> <u>sit</u>.

**To Do Activity**   Punch holes around the borders of the page.   Then, have the child string a piece of yarn or ribbon all the way around to frame the pictures.   Have her describe each picture using a correct sentence.

113

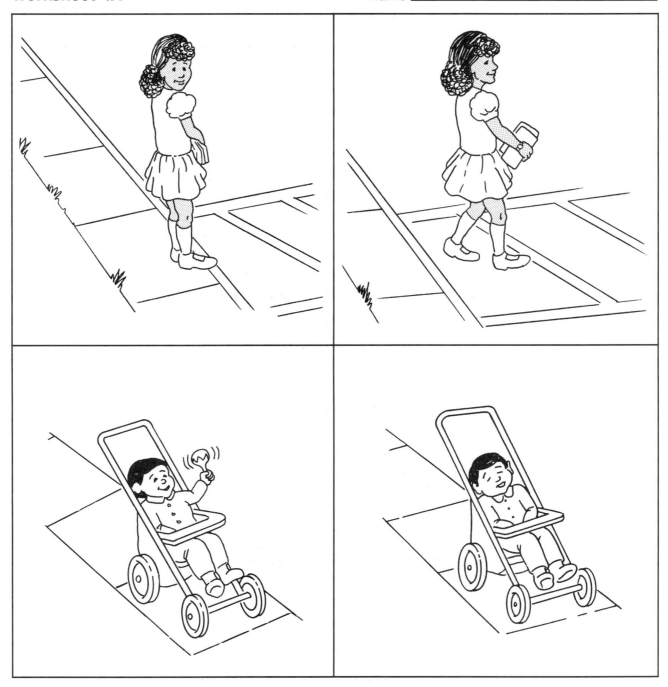

**Expanded Sentence Repetition**  (Point to each picture as you say:)

  Listen.   The girl is standing on the curb.   What will she do next?   Say this:   She will walk across the street.

  Listen.   The baby is playing with his rattle.   What will he do next?   Say this:   He will sleep in the stroller.

**Expanded Sentence Production**  (Point to the first picture in each pair and say,) The girl is standing on the curb. (or) The baby is playing with his rattle. What will she/he do next?  (The child responds with expanded sentences such as:)

  The girl <u>will walk</u> across the street.
  The baby <u>will sleep</u> in the stroller.

**To Do Activity**   Cut out a long, narrow strip of brown construction paper to make a totem pole.   Then, cut out the pictures on this page.   Have the child sequence the pictures and paste a picture on the totem pole after he describes it correctly in an expanded sentence.

114

**Expanded Sentence Repetition**  (Point to each picture as you say:)

    Listen.   The boy is leaving school.   What will he do next?   Say this:   He will run to catch the bus.

    Listen.   The girls are sitting on the ground.   What will they do next?   Say this:   They will play basketball.

**Expanded Sentence Production**   (Point to the first picture in each pair and say,) The boy is leaving school. (or) The girls are sitting on the ground. What will he/they do next?   (The child responds with expanded sentences such as:)

    The boy <u>will</u> <u>run</u> to catch the bus.
    The girls <u>will</u> <u>play</u> basketball.

**To Do Activity**   Cut these pictures out.   Give the child a large piece of construction paper.   Let her make a snowman by pasting each picture on the paper when she describes it correctly in an expanded sentence. Then, have her draw in the winter background and the snowman's arms and scarf.

115

**Expanded Sentence Repetition**   (Point to each picture as you say:)
    Listen.   The girl is tripping on the rock.   What will she do next?   Say this:   She will cry beside the tree.
    Listen.   The painters are putting the ladder up.   What will they do next?   Say this:   They will paint the building.

**Expanded Sentence Production**   (Point to the first picture in each pair and say,)  The girl is tripping on the rock. (or)  The painters are putting the ladder up.   What will she/they do next?   (The child responds with expanded sentences such as:)
    The girl <u>will</u> <u>cry</u> beside the tree.
    The painters <u>will</u> <u>paint</u> the building.

**To Do Activity**   Cut these pictures apart and mount them on pieces of colored construction paper.   Lay the pictures in front of the child.   Then, turn over the second picture in each sequence and ask the child to remember what happened in each picture.   Take turns with the child, telling what is happening and what will happen next in expanded sentences.

116

**Expanded Sentence Repetition**   (Point to each picture as you say:)
   Listen.   The girl is walking to the swing.   What will she do next?   Say this:   She will sit on the swing.
   Listen.   The boys are picking apples.   What will they do next?   Say this:   They will eat the apples.

**Expanded Sentence Production**   (Point to the first picture in each pair and say,) The girl is walking to the swing. (or) The boys are picking apples.   What will she/they do next?   (The child responds with sentences such as:)
   The girl <u>will sit</u> on the swing.
   The boys <u>will eat</u> the apples.

**To Do Activity**   Play Simon Says with the child, taking turns being the leader.   Use future tense in all your commands, starting with the actions on this page.   For example, say, "Simon says you will eat an apple."

# Worksheet 5A: After School

Use this scene with the scene on the next page.

118

**Worksheet 5B: After School**

Use this scene with the scene on the previous page.

119

**Carryover Directions**

Look at these two pictures.  The first picture shows people doing things.  The second picture shows what they do next.  Tell me what the people will do next.  Tell me all about them.  (If the child has difficulty, point to one of the action sequences and ask,) What will the ____ do next? (Continue with the task until the child describes all the action with sentences such as:)

1.  The girl will walk across the street.

2.  The boy will run to the bus.

3.  The child will sleep in the stroller.

4.  The girls will play basketball.

5.  The girl will cry beside the tree.

6.  The men will paint the school.

7.  The girl will sit on the swing.

8.  The boys will eat apples.


**To Do Activity**   Have the child color the people in these scenes.  Then, have her make up a story, telling what each person is doing and what they will do in the next scene.  Encourage the use of expanded sentences, modeling and expanding the child's responses appropriately.

**Worksheet 6A: In the Backyard**

Use this scene with the scene on the next page.

121

**Worksheet 6B:  In the Backyard**

Use this scene with the scene on the previous page.

# Worksheets 6A and 6B:  In the Backyard

## Posttest Directions

Here are some pictures.  The first picture shows people and animals doing things.  The second picture shows what they do next.  Tell me what the people and the animals will do next.  Tell me all about them.  (If the child has difficulty, point to one of the action sequences and ask,)  What will the ___ do next?  (Continue until the child describes all the future action with sentences such as:)

1.  The woman will talk to the man.

2.  The man will cook on the grill.

3.  The boy will ride his big wheel.

4.  The rabbits will hop across the yard.

5.  The girls will dive into the pool.

6.  The woman will dig in the garden.

7.  The girl will climb a tree.

8.  The babies will crawl to the garden.

## To Do Activity

Cut pictures apart from comic strips.  Have the children resequence the pictures and use future sentences to talk about each action which is about to happen.  For extra practice, talk about new endings or predict what will happen after the last picture.

**Worksheet 1: At the Circus**

Prepositions

## Worksheet 1:  At the Circus

**Pretest Directions:  Expressive**

Look at this picture.  It shows people and animals in many different places.  Tell me where each one is.  (Point to each picture and say,) Tell me where the ___ is.  (The child responds with sentences such as:)

1.  The clown is <u>in</u> the car.

2.  The monkey is <u>on</u> the car.

3.  The bear is <u>next to</u> the lion.

4.  The lion tamer is <u>between</u> two lions.

5.  The boy is <u>behind</u> the man.

6.  The man is <u>in front of</u> the boy.

7.  This dog is <u>over</u> the chair.

8.  This dog is <u>under</u> the chair.

**Pretest Directions:  Receptive**

Materials:  red, green, blue, yellow, purple, orange, black, and pink crayons

Let's practice listening carefully.  Look at your worksheet.  I will talk about the things you see and tell you what to do on your worksheet.

1.  Listen.  Pick up your red crayon.  Draw a circle around the person in the car.

2.  Listen.  Pick up your green crayon.  Draw a circle around the animal on the car.

3.  Listen.  Pick up your blue crayon.  Draw a circle around the animal next to the lion.

4.  Listen.  Pick up your yellow crayon.  Draw a circle around the person between two lions.

5.  Listen.  Pick up your purple crayon.  Draw a circle around the person behind the man.

6.  Listen.  Pick up your orange crayon.  Draw a circle around the person in front of the boy.

7.  Listen.  Pick up your black crayon.  Draw a circle around the animal over the chair.

8.  Listen.  Pick up your pink crayon.  Draw a circle around the animal under the chair.

Good listening!

Name _____

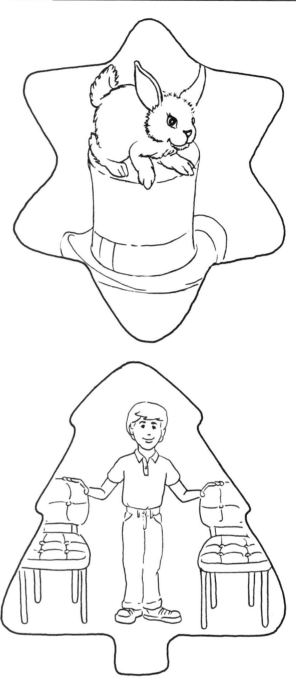

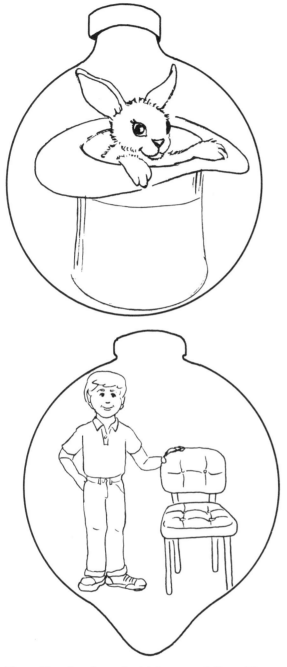

**Auditory Bombardment**   Listen carefully. (Stress the preposition in each sentence as you slowly point to each picture.)
>    The rabbit is in the hat.
>    Now, it is on the hat.
>    The boy is next to the chair.
>    Now, he is between the chairs.

**Auditory Discrimination**   Listen to what I say. Then, point to the picture I talk about.   (Describe the pictures at random.)
>    The rabbit is in the hat.
>    The rabbit is on the hat.
>    The boy is next to the chair.
>    The boy is between the chairs.

**To Do Activity**   Draw the outline of a Christmas tree.   Cut these pictures apart and mount them on pieces of colored construction paper.   Have the child choose the picture you describe and paste it on the tree.

127

Name _____

**Auditory Bombardment**   Listen carefully.   (Stress the preposition in each sentence as you slowly point to each picture.)

> The mouse is behind the cat.
> Now, it is in front of the cat.
> The helicopter is over the bridge.
> Now, it is under the bridge.

**Auditory Discrimination**   Listen to what I say. Then, point to the picture I talk about.   (Describe the pictures at random.)

> The mouse is behind the cat.
> The mouse is in front of the cat.
> The helicopter is over the bridge.
> The helicopter is under the bridge.

**To Do Activity**   Copy two sets of these pictures.   Mount them on stiff paper and cut them apart.   Place the cards face down, mix them up, and play concentration with the child.   Take turns turning over a pair of cards.   Take another turn if you turn over a match.   Describe each picture for the child as it is turned over in the game.

**Sentence Repetition**   Say what I say.   (Point to each picture as you say:)

> The clown is in the car.
> Now, he is on the car.
> The man is next to the lion.
> Now, he is between the lions.

**Sentence Production**   (Point to each picture and ask,) Where is the ____?   (The child responds with sentences such as:)

> The clown is <u>in</u> the car.
> The clown is <u>on</u> the car.
> The man is <u>next to</u> the lion.
> The man is <u>between</u> the lions.

**To Do Activity**   Have a treasure hunt.   Cut these pictures apart and mount them on pieces of construction paper.   Hide them around the room.   If the child finds a picture and describes it correctly in a sentence, he puts it in a sack.   Variation:   Give the child clues using prepositions to find each treasure such as, "It is next to something we write with."

**Sentence Repetition**   Say what I say.   (Point to each picture as you say:)
   The man is in front of the boy.
   Now, he is behind the boy.
   The dog is over the chair.
   Now, it is under the chair.

**Sentence Production**   (Point to each picture and ask,) Where is the ____?   (The child responds with sentences such as:)
   The man is in front of the boy.
   The man is behind the boy.
   The dog is over the chair.
   The dog is under the chair.

**To Do Activity**   Cut these pictures apart and mount them on cards.   Take turns acting out the prepositions from each picture, having the other person describe the action with the appropriate preposition in a complete sentence.

130

**Expanded Sentence Repetition**   Say what I say.
(Point to each picture as you say:)
   The girl is standing next to the teacher.
   The teacher is standing in front of her desk.
   These crayons are on the box.
   These crayons are still in the box.

**Expanded Sentence Production**   (Point to each
picture and ask,) Where is/are the ___?   The child
responds with expanded sentences such as:)
   The girl is standing next to the teacher.
   The teacher is standing in front of her desk.
   These crayons are on the box.
   These crayons are still in the box.

**To Do Activity**   Copy two sets of these pictures.   Cut one set apart and mount both sets on poster board for
a lotto activity.   Place the individual pictures face down on the table.   Have the child pick a card, describe
it in a complete sentence, and match it to her board.

**Worksheet 4B**                          Name _____

**Expanded Sentence Repetition**  Say what I say. (Point to each picture as you say:)

> The boy with glasses is standing between a girl and a boy.
> The girl is standing behind the boy with glasses.
> Two girls are holding hands over the boy.
> The boy is going under their arms.

**Expanded Sentence Production**  (Point to each picture and ask,) Where is/are the ___?  The child responds with expanded sentences such as:)

> The boy with glasses is standing <u>between</u> a girl and a boy.
> The girl is standing <u>behind</u> the boy with glasses.
> Two girls are holding hands <u>over</u> the boy.
> The boy is going <u>under</u> their arms.

**To Do Activity**  Cut these pictures apart and mount them on pieces of construction paper.  Have the child choose a circle and paste it on a piece of paper if he describes the picture correctly in a complete sentence. Have the child paste the circles next to each other in a long line.  When all the pictures are pasted on the paper, draw antennae and some small legs, and you have a caterpillar!

**Worksheet 5: Kindergarten Fun**

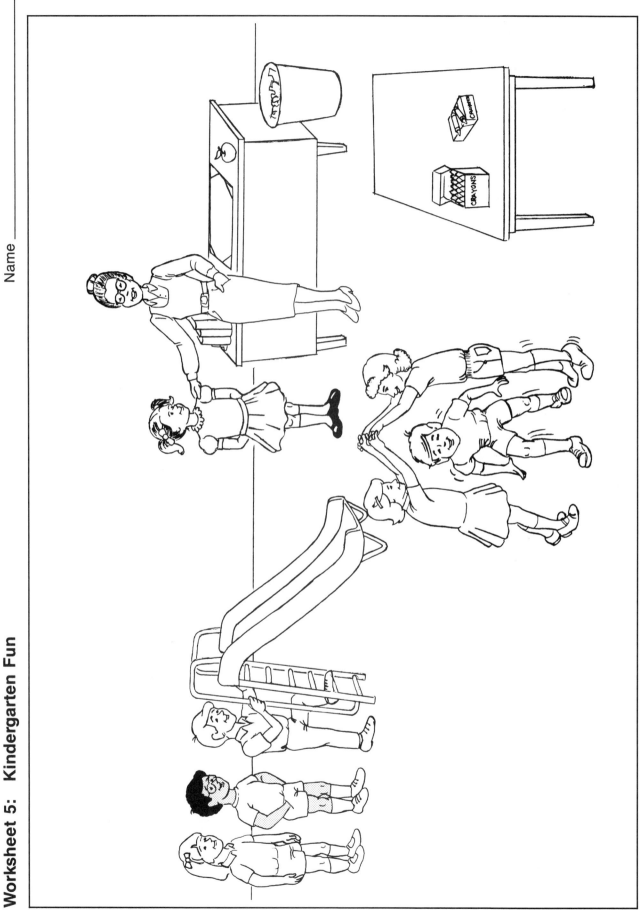

133

# Worksheet 5:   Kindergarten Fun

**Carryover Directions**

Tell me about this picture.   (If the child has difficulty, point to one of the pictures and ask,) Where is/are the ___?   (Continue with the task until the child describes all of the pictures with sentences such as:)

1.   The girl is standing <u>next</u> <u>to</u> the teacher.

2.   The teacher is standing <u>in</u> <u>front</u> <u>of</u> her desk.

3.   Two crayons are <u>on</u> the box.

4.   The other crayons are <u>in</u> the box.

5.   The boy with glasses is standing <u>between</u> a girl and a boy.

6.   The girl is standing <u>behind</u> the boy with glasses.

7.   Two girls are holding hands <u>over</u> the boy.

8.   The boy is going <u>under</u> their arms.

**To Do Activity**

Cut out pictures from magazines demonstrating each of these prepositions.   Make a collage by pasting them on a piece of colored construction paper.   Then, talk about the pictures in complete sentences with the child.   Tell how each picture is placed in relation to the other pictures in the collage.

**Worksheet 6:  Hide 'n' Seek**

135

# Worksheet 6:  Hide 'n' Seek

## Posttest Directions

Here is a picture.  Point to a person or an animal and tell me where it is.  Tell me all about them.
(If the child has difficulty, point to one of the pictures and say,) Tell me about this one.
(Continue until the child uses all the prepositions in sentences such as:)

1.  The boy is hiding <u>in</u> the garbage can.

2.  The cat is sitting <u>on</u> the garbage can.

3.  The girl is counting <u>next to</u> the tree.

4.  The squirrel on the ground is standing
     <u>between</u> the girl and the tree.

5.  The girl is peeking out from <u>behind</u> a tree.

6.  The tree is <u>in front of</u> the girl.

7.  The squirrel is <u>under</u> a nest in the tree.

8.  The nest is <u>over</u> the squirrel.


## To Do Activity

Play Hide 'n' Seek with the child.  Take turns.  The person hiding gives "it" clues using
prepositions in complete sentences.  For example, "I am sitting under something you write on."

**Worksheet 1: In the Backyard**

137

# Worksheet 1:  In the Backyard

**Pretest Directions:  Expressive**

Look at this picture.  Tell me about all the things in the picture.  (If the child has difficulty, point to the different items and say *Tell me about these.*  Try to elicit a response for each item listed below.)

1.  tables

2.  girls

3.  plates

4.  cups

5.  spoons

6.  crayons

7.  boys

8.  dogs

**Pretest Directions:  Receptive**

Materials:  red, blue, green, orange, purple, yellow, pink, and black crayons

Let's practice listening carefully.  Look at your worksheet.  I will talk about the things you see and tell you what to do on your worksheet.  ( . . . indicates a pause.)

1.  Listen.  Pick up your red crayon.  Draw a circle around . . . table.

2.  Listen.  Pick up your blue crayon.  Draw a circle around . . . girls.

3.  Listen.  Pick up your green crayon.  Draw a circle around . . . plates.

4.  Listen.  Pick up your orange crayon.  Draw a circle around . . . cup.

5.  Listen.  Pick up your purple crayon.  Draw a circle around . . . spoon.

6.  Listen.  Pick up your yellow crayon.  Draw a circle around . . . crayons.

7.  Listen.  Pick up your pink crayon.  Draw a circle around . . . boy.

8.  Listen.  Pick up your black crayon.  Draw a circle around . . . dogs.

That's the way to listen!

**Auditory Bombardment**   Listen carefully.   (Point to each picture as you name it.)
    table . . . tables
    girl . . . girls
    plate . . . plates
    cup . . . cups

**Auditory Discrimination**   Listen to what I say. Then, point to the picture I talk about.   (Ask about the pictures at random.)
    Show me the ___ .
    table . . . tables
    girl . . . girls
    plate . . . plates
    cup . . . cups

**To Do Activity**   Cut these pictures apart and mount them on pieces of colored construction paper.   Lay the pictures in front of the child and have him point to the picture you describe.   For each correct answer, have the child put the picture into an empty cracker box.   See how many pictures he can get.

Name _____

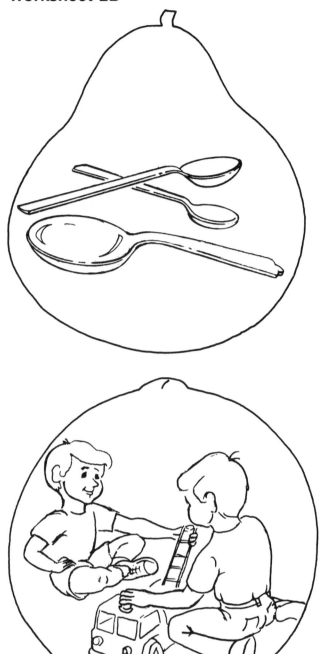

**Auditory Bombardment**   Listen carefully.   (Point to each picture as you name it.)

    spoon . . . spoons
    crayon . . . crayons
    boy . . . boys
    dog . . . dogs

**Auditory Discrimination**   Listen to what I say. Then, point to the picture I talk about.   (Ask about the pictures at random.)

    Show me the ____ .
    spoon . . . spoons
    crayon . . . crayons
    boy . . . boys
    dog . . . dogs

**To Do Activity**   Cut these shapes apart and mount them on pieces of construction paper.   Tie a string to each shape.   Have the child select the picture you describe and tie it to a coat hanger to make a mobile.

140

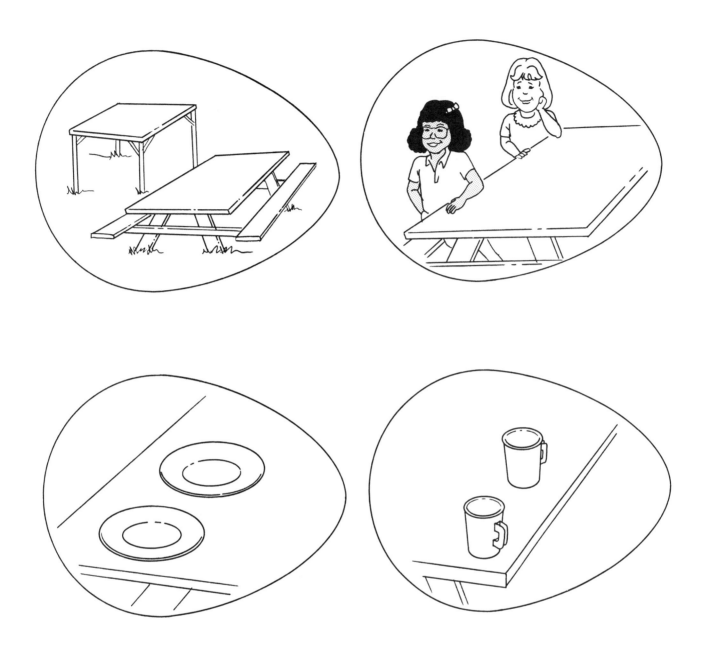

**Word Repetition**  Say what I say.  (Point to each picture as you say:)
  tables
  girls
  plates
  cups

**Word Production**  (Point to each picture and ask,) What are these?  (The child answers with the appropriate response of:)
  tables
  girls
  plates
  cups

**To Do Activity**  Cut these pictures apart and mount them on pieces of colored construction paper.  Draw an Easter basket or use a real wicker basket.  Have the child pick an egg and put it in the Easter basket if he names the picture correctly.

**Word Repetition**   Say what I say.   (Point to each picture as you say:)
    spoons
    crayons
    boys
    dogs

**Word Production**   (Point to each picture and ask,) What are these?   (The child answers with the appropriate response of:)
    spoons
    crayons
    boys
    dogs

**To Do Activity**   Cut these pictures apart and mount them on construction paper.   Place the cards on the floor.   Have the child toss a beanbag at the pictures and name each picture the beanbag lands on.

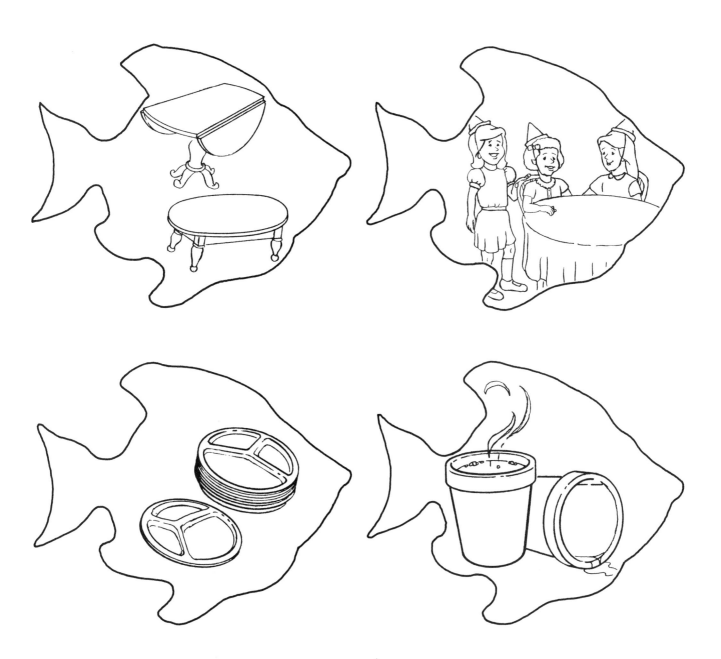

**Sentence Repetition**   Say what I say.   (Point to each picture as you say:)
 These are . . . tables.
                girls.
                plates.
                cups.

**Sentence Production**   (Point to each picture and ask,) What are these?   The child responds with sentences such as:)
 These are . . . tables.
                girls.
                plates.
                cups.

**To Do Activity**   Cut these pictures apart and mount them on pieces of construction paper.   Put a paper clip on each fish and use a fishing pole with a magnet at the end of a string.   Have the child catch fish.   If he can describe the picture using a correct sentence, he keeps it.   See if he can catch all the fish!

**Sentence Repetition** Say what I say. (Point to each picture as you say:)
  These are . . . spoons.
       crayons.
       boys.
       dogs.

**Sentence Production** (Point to each picture and ask,) What are these? The child responds with sentences such as:)
  These are . . . spoons.
       crayons.
       boys.
       dogs.

**To Do Activity** Cut these pictures apart and scatter them on the table. Have the child close her eyes and point to one of the pictures. If she describes the picture using a correct sentence when she opens her eyes, she puts it in her pile. See if she can collect all the pictures!

**Expanded Sentence Repetition**   Say what I say.
(Point to each picture as you say:)
    The tables are long.
    The girls are looking out the window.
    The plates are round.
    The cups are near the plates.

**Expanded Sentence Production**   (Point to each
picture and say,) Tell me about these.   The child
responds with expanded sentences such as:)
    The <u>tables</u> are long.
    The <u>girls</u> are looking out the window.
    The <u>plates</u> are round.
    The <u>cups</u> are near the plates.

**To Do Activity**   Cut these pictures apart and mount them on colored construction paper.   Lay the pictures
face down.   Turn one over, describe it, then place it face down again and mix up the pictures.   Have the
child guess where it is, turn it over, and describe it correctly in a complete sentence.

REGULAR PLURALS                          145

Name _____

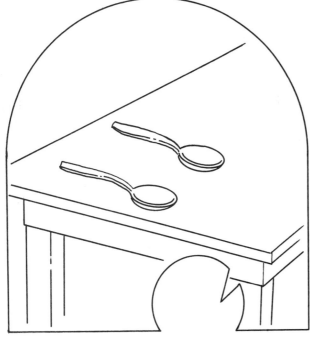

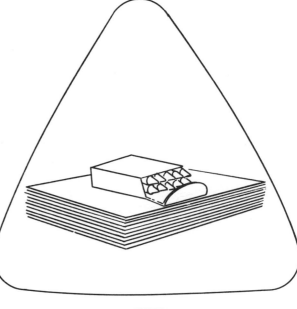

**Expanded Sentence Repetition**   Say what I say.
(Point to each picture as you say:)
   The spoons are on the table.
   The crayons are on the paper.
   The boys are eating lunch.
   The dogs are walking.

**Expanded Sentence Production**   (Point to each picture and say,) Tell me about these.   The child responds with expanded sentences such as:)
   The <u>spoons</u> are on the table.
   The <u>crayons</u> are on the paper.
   The <u>boys</u> are eating lunch.
   The <u>dogs</u> are walking.

**To Do Activity**   Cut these pictures apart and mount them on colored construction paper.   Draw a large outline of a pumpkin or cut one out of orange poster board.   Have the child choose the picture you name and paste it on the jack-o'-lantern.   Then, have the child describe the picture with a complete sentence.

146

**Worksheet 6: In the Cafeteria**

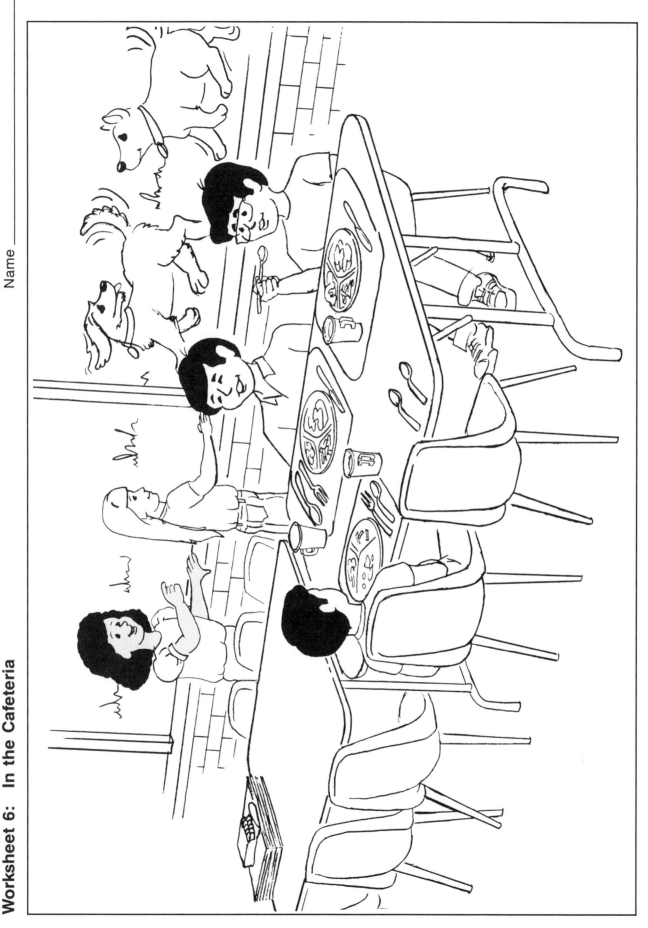

# Worksheet 6: In the Cafeteria

## Carryover Directions

Tell me about this picture.   (If the child has difficulty, point to one of the pictures and say,) Tell me about these.   (Continue until the child uses all the plurals in sentences such as:)

1.   The <u>tables</u> are long.

2.   The <u>girls</u> are looking out the window.

3.   The <u>plates</u> are round.

4.   The <u>cups</u> are near the plates.

5.   The <u>spoons</u> are on the table.

6.   The <u>crayons</u> are on the paper.

7.   The <u>boys</u> are eating lunch.

8.   The <u>dogs</u> are walking.

## To Do Activity

Have the child color the plural items on his worksheet.   Then, help him make a booklet by cutting out these pictures and other pictures from magazines and catalogs and pasting them on the pages of the booklet.   Then, talk about the pictures and write a complete sentence below each one.

**Worksheet 7: In the Classroom**

149

# Worksheet 7: In the Classroom

## Posttest Directions

Here is a new picture. Tell me about all the things on this page. Tell me everything you can. (If the child has difficulty, point to one of the groups of items and say,) Tell me about these. (Continue until the child uses all the plurals in sentences such as:)

1. The <u>books</u> are on the teacher's desk.

2. There are some <u>desks</u> in the room.

3. The <u>windows</u> are large.

4. The <u>coats</u> are hanging on hooks.

5. The <u>lights</u> are on the ceiling.

6. The <u>pencils</u> are on the desk.

7. The <u>numbers</u> are on the chalkboard.

8. The <u>letters</u> of the alphabet are above the chalkboard.

## To Do Activity

Let the child color the plural items on her worksheet. Then, cut the groups of items apart and paste them on cards. Select one of the cards and describe it incorrectly. Let the child roleplay the teacher and correct your sentence.

Name _____

**Worksheet 1: At the Fair**

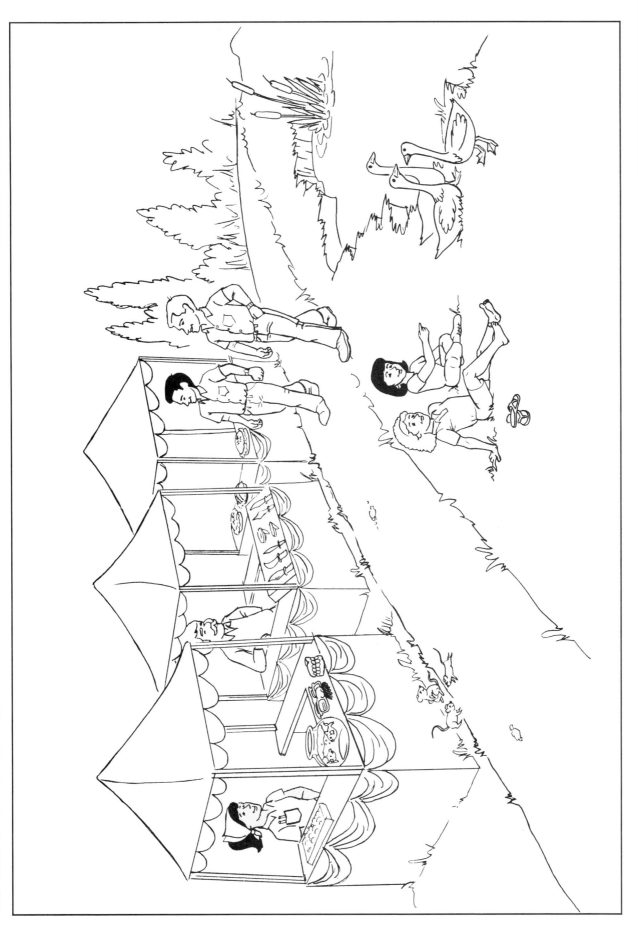

151

# Worksheet 1: At the Fair

**Pretest Directions: Expressive**

Look at this picture. Tell me about all the things in the picture. (If the child has difficulty, point to each plural item and say,) Tell me about these. (Continue until the child uses all the plurals listed below:)

1. feet

2. mice

3. geese

4. teeth

5. men

6. women

7. knives

8. fish

**Pretest Directions: Receptive**

Materials: black, yellow, orange, purple, red, pink, green, and blue crayons

Let's practice listening carefully. Look at your worksheet. I will talk about the things you see and tell you what to do on your worksheet. ( . . . indicates a pause.)

1. Listen. Pick up your black crayon. Draw a circle around . . . feet.

2. Listen. Pick up your yellow crayon. Draw a circle around . . . knife.

3. Listen. Pick up your orange crayon. Draw a circle around . . . geese.

4. Listen. Pick up your purple crayon. Draw a circle around . . . fish.

5. Listen. Pick up your red crayon. Draw a circle around . . . man.

6. Listen. Pick up your pink crayon. Draw a circle around . . . women.

7. Listen. Pick up your green crayon. Draw a circle around . . . mouse.

8. Listen. Pick up your blue crayon. Draw a circle around . . . teeth.

Nice work!

**Auditory Bombardment** Listen carefully. (Point to each picture as you name it.)
 foot . . . feet
 mouse . . . mice
 goose . . . geese
 tooth . . . teeth

**Auditory Discrimination** Listen to what I say. Then, point to the picture I talk about. (Ask about the pictures at random.)
 Show me the ____ .
 foot . . . feet
 mouse . . . mice
 goose . . . geese
 tooth . . . teeth

**To Do Activity** Make a plurals mobile. Have the child color the pictures and then cut them apart. Mount the pictures on heavier paper and tie a piece of yarn to each picture. Then, lay all the pictures in front of the child and name the singular and plural of each picture at random. If the child points to the correct picture, let him tie it to a hanger to make his mobile.

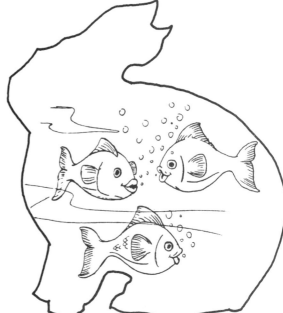

**Auditory Bombardment**   Listen carefully.   (Point to each picture as you name it.)

   man . . . men
   woman . . . women
   knife . . . knives
   fish . . . fish

**Auditory Discrimination**   Listen to what I say. Then, point to the picture I talk about.   (Ask about the pictures at random.)

   Show me the ___ .
   man . . . men
   woman . . . women
   knife . . . knives
   fish . . . fish

**To Do Activity**   Cut these pictures apart and mount them on construction paper.   Have cotton balls and glue ready for the child.   Then, with the pictures in front of him, ask the child to point to the picture you name.   Let him glue on a cotton ball for the bunny's tail if he identifies the picture correctly.

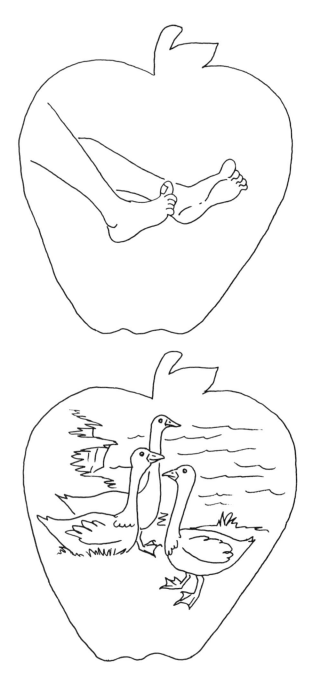
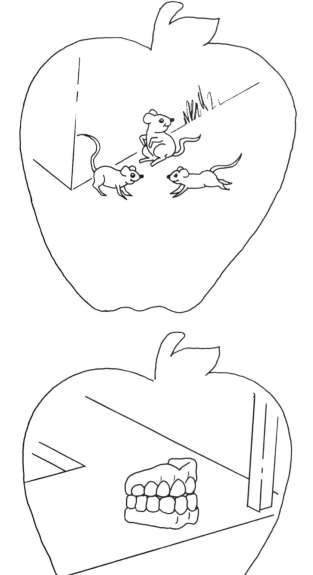

**Word Repetition**   Say what I say.   (Point to each picture as you say:)
   feet
   mice
   geese
   teeth

**Word Production**   (Point to each picture and ask,) What are these?   (The child answers with the appropriate response of:)
   feet
   mice
   geese
   teeth

**To Do Activity**   Draw the outline of a tree.   Then, cut these pictures apart and mount them on construction paper.   Have the child choose an apple and paste it on the tree if he describes the picture correctly.

Name _____

**Word Repetition**   Say what I say.   (Point to each picture as you say:)

men
women
knives
fish

**Word Production**   (Point to each picture and ask,) What are these?   (The child answers with the appropriate response of:)

men
women
knives
fish

**To Do Activity**   Copy two sets of these pictures.   Cut one set apart and mount both sets on poster board so you can play lotto.   Place the individual pictures face down on the table.   Next, have the child pick a card and match it to her board if she describes the picture correctly.

156

Name _____

**Sentence Repetition**   Say what I say.   (Point to each picture as you say:)
   These are . . . feet.
                mice.
                geese.
                teeth.

**Sentence Production**   (Point to each picture and ask,) What are these?   (The child responds with sentences such as:)
   These are . . . feet.
                mice.
                geese.
                teeth.

**To Do Activity**   Cut these pictures apart and mount them on construction paper.   Decorate a shoe box to look like a barn.   Have the child describe the pictures in complete sentences.   Then, she can put them in the barn.

IRREGULAR PLURALS

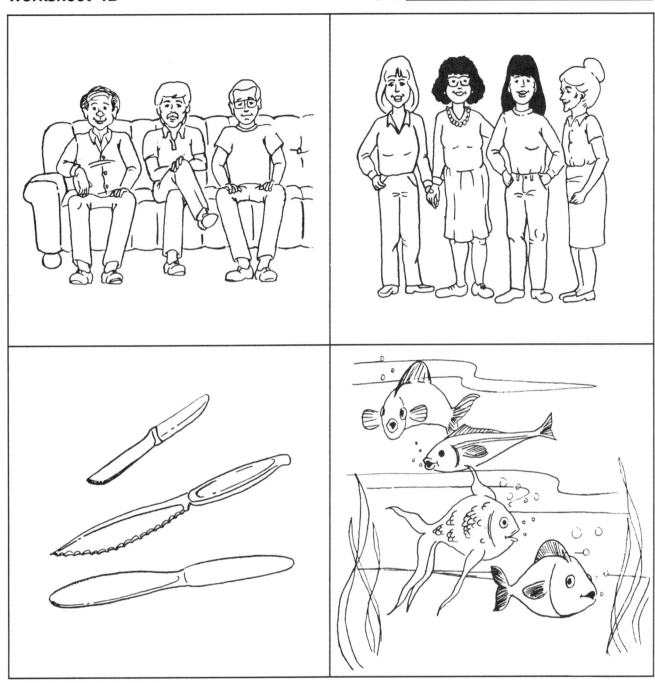

**Sentence Repetition**   Say what I say.   (Point to each picture as you say:)
   These are . . . men.
                        women.
                        knives.
                        fish.

**Sentence Production**   (Point to each picture and ask,) What are these?   (The child responds with sentences such as:)
   These are . . . men.
                        women.
                        knives.
                        fish.

**To Do Activity**   Copy two sets of these pictures.   Mount them on stiff paper and cut them apart.   Place the cards face down, mix them up, and play concentration with the child.   Take turns turning over a pair of cards and describing each of them in complete sentences.   Take another turn if you turn over a match.

158

**Expanded Sentence Repetition**   Say what I say.
(Point to each picture as you say:)
   The boy's feet are bare.
   The mice are in a cage.
   The geese are on leashes.
   The teeth are big.

**Expanded Sentence Production**   (Point to each
picture and say,) Tell me about these.   (The child
responds with expanded sentences such as:)
   The boy's <u>feet</u> are bare.
   The <u>mice</u> are in a cage.
   The <u>geese</u> are on leashes.
   The <u>teeth</u> are big.

**To Do Activity**   Have a treasure hunt.   Cut these pictures apart and mount them on paper.   Hide them
around the room.   If the child finds a picture and describes it correctly in a complete sentence, let her put
it in a sack.   See if she can find all the treasures!

**Expanded Sentence Repetition**   Say what I say.
(Point to each picture as you say:)
   The men are sitting by the door.
   The women are sitting on the couch.
   The knives are in the picture.
   The fish are in the bowl.

**Expanded Sentence Production**   (Point to each
picture and say,)  Tell me about these.   (The child
responds with expanded sentences such as:)
   The <u>men</u> are sitting by the door.
   The <u>women</u> are sitting on the couch.
   The <u>knives</u> are in the picture.
   The <u>fish</u> are in the bowl.

**To Do Activity**   Cut these pictures apart and paste them on cards.   Choose one of the cards and describe
it incorrectly in a sentence.   Let the child play teacher and correct your sentence.

160

Name _____

# Worksheet 6:   At the Veterinarian's Office

## Carryover Directions

Tell me about this picture.   (If the child has difficulty, point to one of the pictures and say,)  Tell me about these.   (Continue until the child uses all the plurals in sentences such as:)

1.   The <u>women</u> are sitting on the sofa.

2.   The <u>geese</u> are on the floor.

3.   The boy's <u>feet</u> are bare.

4.   The boy has three <u>fish</u> in his fishbowl.

5.   The <u>men</u> are sitting by the door.

6.   There are <u>mice</u> in the cage.

7.   There are many <u>knives</u> in the picture.

8.   The dog has big <u>teeth</u>.

## To Do Activity

Let the child help make a bulletin board of plurals.   Have the child color this picture first.   Then, help her cut them apart and put them on the bulletin board.   Next, look through magazines together and cut out other pictures of these plurals to add to the bulletin board.   Have the child tell a complete sentence about each picture.

## Worksheet 7:  At the Art Fair

163

# Worksheet 7: At the Art Fair

## Posttest Directions

Here is a new picture.  Tell me about all the things on this page.  Tell me everything you can.
(If the child has difficulty, point to one of the items and say,) Tell me about these.  (Continue until the child uses all the plurals in sentences such as:)

1.  The <u>women</u> are looking at the pictures.

2.  The <u>men</u> are sitting on the park bench.

3.  The girl is feeding the <u>geese</u>.

4.  The <u>knives</u> are on the table.

5.  The girl is brushing her <u>teeth</u>.

6.  The <u>fish</u> are jumping back in the water.

7.  The <u>mice</u> are eating cheese.

8.  This man has roller skates on his <u>feet</u>.

## To Do Activity

Talk about each of these plural items as the child colors it.  See how many things you can say about each one.  For example, for the sentence, *The women are looking at the pictures,* say, *What else are the women doing?*  Take turns telling more about each plural item until you and the child have exhausted the possibilities.  Feel free to give the child question prompts such as, *Are the women wearing shoes?*

**Worksheet 1: Ice-Skating**

# Worksheet 1:   Ice-Skating

## Pretest Directions:   Expressive

Look at this picture.   Tell me about all the things in the picture.   (Point out Jeff and Annette by name to the child.   If the child has difficulty, point to each item and label it.   For example, say,) This boy has a hat.   Whose hat is it?   (Continue until the child uses every possessive noun listed below:)

1. boy's hat

2. girl's ice skates

3. Jeff's scarf

4. Annette's mittens

5. dog's paws

6. cat's bow

7. woman's purse

8. man's coat

## Pretest Directions:   Receptive

Materials:   purple, pink, red, blue, green, orange, black, and yellow crayons

Let's practice listening carefully.   Look at your worksheet.   (Point out Jeff and Annette by name to the child.)   I will talk about the things you see and tell you what to do on your worksheet.

1. Listen.   Pick up your purple crayon.   Draw an X on the boy's hat.

2. Listen.   Pick up your pink crayon.   Draw an X on the girl's ice skates.

3. Listen.   Pick up your red crayon.   Draw an X on Jeff's scarf.

4. Listen.   Pick up your blue crayon.   Draw an X on Annette's mittens.

5. Listen.   Pick up your green crayon.   Draw an X on the dog's paws.

6. Listen.   Pick up your orange crayon.   Draw an X on the cat's bow.

7. Listen.   Pick up your black crayon.   Draw an X on the woman's purse.

8. Listen.   Pick up your yellow crayon.   Draw an X on the man's coat.

Good listening!

**Auditory Bombardment**　Listen carefully.　(Point to each picture, stressing the possessive noun as you name it.)

　　the boy's airplane
　　the girl's yo-yo
　　Jeff's pencil
　　Annette's new dress

**Auditory Discrimination**　Listen to what I say. Then, point to the picture I talk about.　(Ask about the pictures at random.)

　　Show me . . . the boy's airplane.
　　　　　　　　the girl's yo-yo.
　　　　　　　　Jeff's pencil.
　　　　　　　　Annette's new dress.

**To Do Activity**　Have the child color these pictures and cut them apart.　Mount the pictures on construction paper.　Next, lay the pictures on the table in front of the child and name one of the items.　If he points to the correct picture let him place it in an empty Kleenex box.　See if he can collect all the pictures.

**Auditory Bombardment**   Listen carefully.   (Point to each picture as you name it.)
   the dog's toy
   the cat's collar
   the woman's car
   the man's cane

**Auditory Discrimination**   Listen to what I say. Then, point to the picture I talk about.   (Ask about the pictures at random.)
   Show me . . . the dog's toy.
                 the cat's collar.
                 the woman's car.
                 the man's cane.

**To Do Activity**   Cut these pictures apart and mount them on construction paper.   Put a paper clip on each fish and use a fishing pole with a magnet at the end of a string.   Have the child catch the fish with the picture you describe.   Let her keep the fish if she is correct.   See if she can catch all the fish!

168

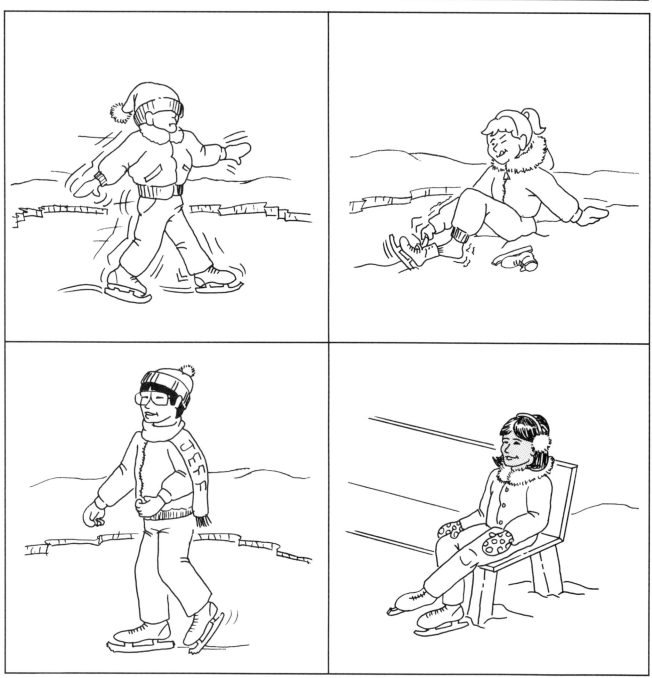

**Phrase Repetition**  Say what I say.  (Point to each picture as you say:)
    the boy's hat
    the girl's ice skates
    Jeff's scarf
    Annette's mittens

**Phrase Production**  (Point to each picture and ask,) What is this? (or) What are these?  (The child answers with the appropriate response of:)
    the <u>boy's</u> hat
    the <u>girl's</u> ice skates
    <u>Jeff's</u> scarf
    <u>Annette's</u> mittens

**To Do Activity**  Number each picture.  Have the child spin a spinner with the numbers one through four. Have him describe the appropriate picture for whichever number the arrow lands on.

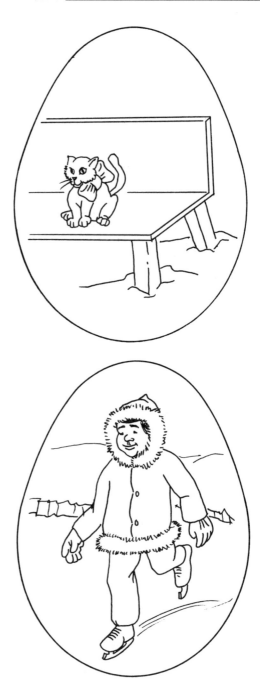

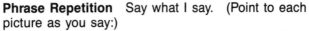

**Phrase Repetition**   Say what I say.   (Point to each picture as you say:)
   the dog's paws
   the cat's bow
   the woman's purse
   the man's coat

**Phrase Production**   (Point to each picture and ask,) What is this? (or) What are these?   (The child answers with the appropriate response of:)
   the <u>dog's</u> paws
   the <u>cat's</u> bow
   the <u>woman's</u> purse
   the <u>man's</u> coat

**To Do Activity**   Cut these pictures apart and mount them on colored construction paper.   Draw an Easter basket or use a wicker basket.   Have the child choose an egg, color it, and put it in the Easter basket if he describes the picture correctly.

170

**Sentence Repetition**　Say what I say.　(Point to each picture as you say:)

　This is . . . the boy's stereo.
　　　　　　the girl's perfume.
　　　　　　Jeff's belt.
　　　　　　Annette's cake.

**Sentence Production**　(Point to each picture and ask,) What is this? (or) What are these?　(The child responds with sentences such as:)

　This is . . . the <u>boy's</u> stereo.
　　　　　　the <u>girl's</u> perfume.
　　　　　　<u>Jeff's</u> belt.
　　　　　　<u>Annette's</u> cake.

**To Do Activity**　Cut these pictures apart and mount them on construction paper.　Draw a tree on a separate piece of paper.　Then, have the child choose a leaf and paste it on the tree if she uses a correct sentence to describe the picture.

**Sentence Repetition**   Say what I say.   (Point to each picture as you say:)
   This is the dog's stick.
   This is the cat's mouse.
   These are the woman's books.
   This is the man's bicycle.

**Sentence Production**   (Point to each picture and ask,) What is this? (or) What are these?   (The child responds with sentences such as:)
   This is the dog's stick.
   This is the cat's mouse.
   These are the woman's books.
   This is the man's bicycle.

**To Do Activity**   Cut these pictures apart and mount them on colored construction paper.   Lay the pictures face down.   Turn one over and use a sentence to describe it.   Then, place it face down again and mix up the pictures.   Have the child guess where it is, turn it over, and describe it correctly in a sentence.

172

Name _____

**Expanded Sentence Repetition**  Say what I say. (Point to each picture as you say:)

The boy's baseball is on the ground.
The girl's glove is too big.
Jeff's tent is falling down.
Annette's doll is very small.

**Expanded Sentence Production**  (Point to each picture and use a wh-question prompt.  For example, ask,) Whose baseball is on the ground? (The child responds with expanded sentences such as:)

The <u>boy's</u> baseball is on the ground.
The <u>girl's</u> glove is too big.
<u>Jeff's</u> tent is falling down.
<u>Annette's</u> doll is very small.

**To Do Activity**  Cut these pictures apart and mount them on colored construction paper.  Take turns describing each picture using an expanded sentence.  See how many different sentences you and the child can make for each possessive noun.  Write the sentences on the back of the tents.

POSSESSIVE NOUNS

**Expanded Sentence Repetition**   Say what I say.
(Point to each picture as you say:)
   The dog's bone is big.
   The cat's bowl is upside down.
   The woman's flashlight is under the bench.
   The man's saw is sharp.

**Expanded Sentence Production**   (Point to each
picture and use a wh-question prompt.   For
example, ask,)  Whose bone is big?   (The child
responds with expanded sentences such as:)
   The <u>dog's</u> bone is big.
   The <u>cat's</u> bowl is upside down.
   The <u>woman's</u> flashlight is under the bench.
   The <u>man's</u> saw is sharp.

**To Do Activity**   Cut these pictures apart and mount them on colored construction paper.   Describe a
picture, using an incorrect possessive noun in your sentence.   Let the child color the object that belongs to
the noun in that picture if he says the sentence correctly.

174

**Worksheet 6: Camping**

## Worksheet 6:   Camping

### Carryover Directions

Tell me about all the things in this picture.   Tell me who has the different things.   (If the child has difficulty, point to one of the pictures and say,) Tell me about this.   (Continue until the child uses all the possessive nouns in sentences such as:)

1.   The boy's baseball is on the ground.

2.   The girl's glove is too big.

3.   Jeff's tent is falling down.

4.   Annette's doll is very small.

5.   The dog's bone is big.

6.   The cat's bowl is upside down.

7.   The woman's flashlight is under the picnic bench.

8.   The man's saw is very sharp.

### To Do Activity

Mount these pictures on poster board and cut them apart in jigsaw fashion to make eight large pieces.   Have the child color the pictures.   Next, have the child describe each of the pictures using correct sentences.   Then, she can put the puzzle back together.

**Worksheet 7:  At the Library**

# Worksheet 7: At the Library

**Posttest Directions**

Here is a new picture.  Tell me about all the things on the page.  Tell me who has the different things.  (Point out and name each of the people.  If the child has difficulty, point to an item and say,)  Tell me about this.  (Continue until the child uses all the possessive nouns in sentences such as:)

1.  The <u>librarian's</u> glasses are broken.

2.  The <u>student's</u> backpack is heavy.

3.  The <u>baby's</u> toy is on the floor.

4.  The <u>child's</u> robot has a broken leg.

5.  <u>Mary's</u> books are piled on the table.

6.  <u>Brad's</u> arm is in a cast.

7.  The <u>bird's</u> nest is in the tree.

8.  The <u>squirrel's</u> acorn is large.

**To Do Activity**

Have the child bring in his favorite picture book.  Look through the pictures with the child and see how many possessive nouns he can use correctly in expanded sentences.  For correct responses, give the child tokens to be turned in later for a prize.

**Worksheet 1:  At the Swimming Pool**

# Worksheet 1: At the Swimming Pool

**Pretest Directions:  Expressive**

Look at this picture.  Everyone brought different things to the swimming pool.  Tell me whose things are here.  (Point to the girl's sunglasses.)  Whose sunglasses are these?  (The child answers, *These are her sunglasses.*)  Now, tell me about the other things in the picture.  Show me which thing you're talking about.  (If the child has difficulty, point to different objects and ask *Whose ___ is/are this/these?*  Continue with the task until the child uses all the possessive pronouns in sentences such as:)

1.  This is her hat.

2.  This is his whistle.

3.  These are their ice cream cones.

4.  This is its bone.

5.  This is his towel.

(To elicit the pronouns *my, our,* and *your,* have the child roleplay.  For example, say,) Pretend you are this man.  (Point to the lifeguard.)  What do you say to show someone your whistle?  (The child answers, *Look at my whistle.*  Then, say,)  Pretend we are these people eating ice cream cones.  Whose ice cream cones are they?  (The child answers, *They're our ice cream cones.*  Next, say,)  Pretend this dog belongs to me.  Whose dog is it?  (The child answers, *It's your dog.*)

**Pretest Directions:  Receptive**

Materials:   red, blue, brown, green, and orange crayons

Let's practice listening carefully.  Look at your worksheet.  I will talk about the things everyone brought to the swimming pool and tell you what to do on your worksheet.

1.  Listen.  Find the mother.  Color her hat red.

2.  Listen.  Find the lifeguard.  Draw a blue X on his whistle.

3.  Listen.  Find two girls sitting together.  Color their hair brown.

4.  Listen.  Find the dog.  Draw a green circle around its bone.

5.  Listen.  Find the boy.  Color his towel orange.

6.  Listen.  Draw a red line under your name.

Nice listening!

**Auditory Bombardment**　Listen carefully.　(Stress the pronoun in each picture as you point to the object described.)

　his bicycle
　her comb
　its cage
　their balloons

**Auditory Discrimination**　Listen to what I say. Then, point to the picture I talk about.　(Describe the pictures at random.)

　his bicycle
　her comb
　its cage
　their balloons

(For the pronouns *my, our* and *your*, roleplay.　For example, say,) Pretend this bird belongs to me.　It's my bird.)

**To Do Activity**　Cut out a large heart from construction paper.　Next, cut these pictures out and paste them on construction paper.　Then, have the child choose the picture you describe and paste it on the large heart.

POSSESSIVE PRONOUNS　　　　　　181

**Auditory Bombardment**   Listen carefully. (Stress the pronoun in each picture as you point to the object described.)
   their bike
   its nest
   his sled
   her ring

**Auditory Discrimination**   Listen to what I say. Then, point to the picture I talk about.   (Describe the pictures at random.)
   their bike
   its nest
   his sled
   her ring

(For the pronouns *my, our* and *your,* roleplay.   For example, say,) Now, pretend this ring belongs to me. This is my ring.

**To Do Activity**   Have the child color the pictures.   Then, cut them apart and mount them on construction paper.   Place the pictures on the floor or a table.   Have the child toss buttons onto the pictures as you describe them.

182

**Phrase Repetition**   Say what I say.   (Point to each picture as you say:)

   his towel
   her hat
   their beach ball
   its bone

**Phrase Production**   (Point to each picture and ask,) Whose ____ is this?   (The child answers with the appropriate response of:)

   <u>his</u> towel
   <u>her</u> hat
   <u>their</u> beach ball
   <u>its</u> bone

(For the pronouns *my, our* and *your,* roleplay with the child.   For example, say,) Pretend this dog belongs to you.   Whose dog is it?   (The child answers, *my dog.*)

**To Do Activity**   Mount these pictures on cardboard and cut them apart to make individual pizza pieces. Let the child choose a piece, describe it with a possessive pronoun phrase, and add his pieces together to make a whole pizza.

**Phrase Repetition**   Say what I say.   (Point to each picture as you say:)
   their ice cream cones
   her sunglasses
   his whistle
   its paw

**Phrase Production**   (Point to each picture and ask,) Whose ____ is this? (or) Whose ____ are these?   (The child answers with the appropriate response of:)
   their ice cream cones
   her sunglasses
   his whistle
   its paw

(For the pronouns *my, our* and *your,* roleplay with the child.   For example, say,) Pretend these sunglasses belong to me.   Whose sunglasses are they?   (The child answers, *your sunglasses.*)

**To Do Activity**   Cut out a long, narrow strip of brown construction paper to make a totem pole.   Then, cut out the pictures on this page.   Have the child paste a picture on the totem pole after she describes it correctly in a phrase.

**Sentence Repetition**   Say what I say.   (Point to each picture as you say:)
   This is his newspaper.
   This is her lunch box.
   This is its doghouse.
   This is their game.

**Sentence Production**   (Point to each picture and ask,) Whose ____ is this? (or) Whose ____ are these?   The child responds with sentences such as:)
   This is <u>his</u> newspaper.
   This is <u>her</u> lunch box.
   This is <u>its</u> doghouse.
   This is <u>their</u> game.

(For the pronouns *my, our* and *your,* roleplay with the child.   For example, say,) Pretend this lunch box belongs to us.   Whose lunch box is it?   (The child answers, *It's <u>our</u> lunch box.*)

**To Do Activity**   Place a piece of sandpaper under this page.   Have the child color each picture after he describes it correctly in a sentence.   The sandpaper will give the picture a textured look.

Name _____

**Sentence Repetition**   Say what I say.   (Point to each picture as you say:)
  These are their dogs.
  This is its banana.
  This is his shirt.
  This is her crib.

**Sentence Production**   (Point to each picture and ask,) Whose ___ is this? (or) Whose ___ are these?   The child responds with sentences such as:)
  These are their dogs.
  This is its banana.
  This is his shirt.
  This is her crib.

(For the pronouns *my, our* and *your,* roleplay with the child.   For example, say,) Pretend this shirt belongs to you.   Whose shirt is it?   (The child answers, *It's my shirt.*)

**To Do Activity**   Have the child color the shapes.   Then, cut the shapes out and paste them on a piece of construction paper.   Have the child draw a stem and leaves to finish each flower after she describes it correctly in a sentence.

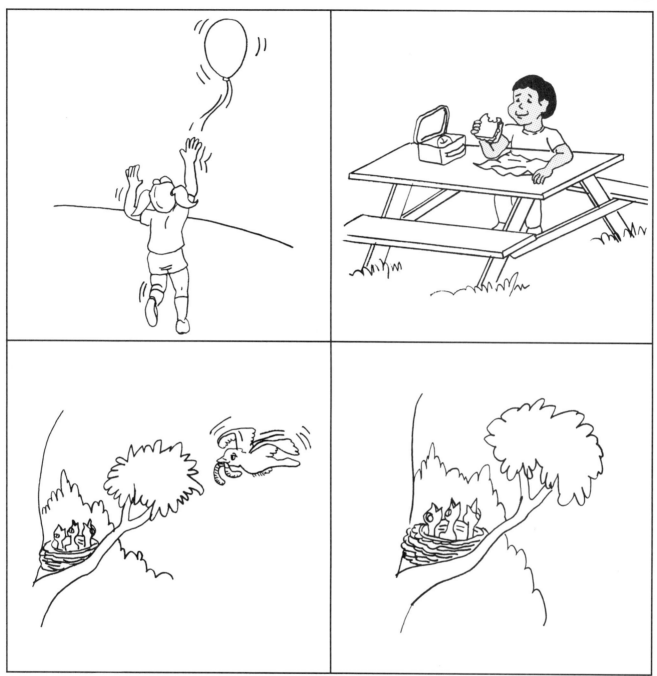

**Expanded Sentence Repetition**   Say what I say.
(Point to each picture as you say:)
  Her balloon is flying away.
  The boy is eating his lunch.
  The bird is flying to its nest.
  The baby birds are in their nest.

**Expanded Sentence Production**   (Point to each picture and ask a wh-question such as,) Whose balloon is flying away?   (The child responds with expanded sentences such as:)
  <u>Her</u> balloon is flying away.
  The boy is eating <u>his</u> lunch.
  The bird is flying to <u>its</u> nest.
  The baby birds are in <u>their</u> nest.

(For the pronouns *my, our* and *your,* roleplay with the child.   For example, say,) Pretend this is my balloon.
Tell me what's happening to it.   (The child answers, <u>*Your*</u> *balloon is flying away.*)

**To Do Activity**   Make two copies of these pictures.   Cut them apart and mount them on poster board cards.
Shuffle the cards and deal them out.   Take turns drawing a card from the other person.   Lay down a pair
after using a correct expanded sentence to describe the picture.

POSSESSIVE PRONOUNS                187

**Expanded Sentence Repetition**   Say what I say.
(Point to each picture as you say:)
    The dog is wagging its tail.
    The girl is riding her bicycle.
    The men are taking their shoes off.
    The police officer is riding his horse.

**Expanded Sentence Production**   (Point to each picture and ask a wh-question such as,) What is the dog wagging?   (The child responds with expanded sentences such as:)
    The dog is wagging <u>its</u> tail.
    The girl is riding <u>her</u> bicycle.
    The men are taking <u>their</u> shoes off.
    The police officer is riding <u>his</u> horse.

(For the pronouns *my, our* and *your,* roleplay with the child.   For example, say,) Pretend this horse belongs to us.   What are you riding?   (The child answers, *I'm riding <u>our</u> horse.*)

**To Do Activity**   Cut these shapes out.   Place a piece of construction paper in front of you.   Have the child describe each picture with an expanded sentence.   For each correct sentence, she can paste the shapes onto the paper to make an ice cream cone.

188

**Worksheet 6: Holiday at the Park**

# Worksheet 6: Holiday at the Park

## Carryover Directons

Look at this picture. People are having fun at the park. Let's talk about the things we can see. (If the child has difficulty, use a prompt. For example, say,) Tell me about the police officer's horse. (Continue with the task until the child uses all the possessive pronouns in sentences such as:)

1. Her balloon is flying away.

2. She's riding her bike.

3. The dog is wagging its tail.

4. The baby birds are in their nest.

5. The mother bird is flying to its nest.

6. The men are taking off their shoes.

7. The police officer is riding his horse.

8. The boy is eating his lunch.

(For the pronouns *my, our* and *your,* roleplay with the child and say,) What is this girl saying? (The child answers, *My balloon is flying away.*) Let's pretend you and your family are bringing something to the park. Tell me about what you're going to bring. (The child answers, *We'll bring our dog to the park.*) Now, tell me what I could bring to the park. (The child answers, *You could bring your picnic basket.*)

**To Do Activity**   Cut the picture into eight pieces like a jigsaw puzzle. Each piece should represent one of the possessive pronouns. Have the child describe the pictures with expanded sentences using the appropriate possessive pronouns as he puts the pieces back together. Have him roleplay some of the characters to use the pronouns *my, our* and *your.*

**Worksheet 7:  Christmas Day**

191

# Worksheet 7:   Christmas Day

## Posttest Directions

Look at this picture.   This family is celebrating Christmas.   Tell me about what you see.   (If the child has difficulty, point to an item and give a prompt.   For example, say,) Tell me about this man's slippers.   (Continue until the child uses all the possessive pronouns in sentences such as:)

1.   <u>His</u> slippers are too big.

2.   <u>Her</u> sweater is too small.

3.   The cat has a bow on <u>its</u> tail.

4.   They like <u>their</u> TV.

5.   She has bows in <u>her</u> hair.

6.   <u>His</u> robot is broken.

7.   <u>Its</u> cage has a wheel.

8.   There are presents in <u>their</u> stockings.

(To elicit the pronouns *my, our* and *your,* roleplay with the child.   Tell her you can each choose your own presents from the picture.   Choose your presents.   Then, talk about your presents with each other.   For example, say,) This is my sweater.   Tell me something about my sweater.   (The child answers, <u>*Your sweater is very small.*</u>)   Now, tell me about your presents.   (The child answers, *This is <u>my</u> hamster.*)   Let's pretend these stockings belong to us.   Tell me about them.   (The child answers, *We have lots of stuff in <u>our</u> stockings.*)

**To Do Activity**   Play a game of Simon Says with the child, pointing to different items in the picture.   Take turns giving commands, using the possessive pronouns given above.   For example, say, "Simon says color their stockings."   In addition, for the pronouns *my, our* and *your,* roleplay with the child, pretending to be one of the people in the picture.

**Worksheet 1: At the Party**

## Worksheet 1:  At the Party

**Pretest Directions:  Expressive**

Look at this picture.  The children are having fun at a birthday party.  Tell me something else about them.  (The child answers, *They are laughing.*  If the child has difficulty, use a wh-question prompt.  For example, ask,) Who can't see?  (Continue with the task until the child uses all the subjective pronouns in sentences such as:)

1.  <u>He</u> can't see.

2.  <u>It</u> is on the wall.

3.  <u>She</u> is taking a picture.

4.  <u>It</u> is on the table.

5.  <u>They</u> are playing a game.

(To elicit the pronouns *we, I,* and *you,* have the child roleplay.  For example, say,) Pretend you are this girl.  (Point to the girl who is pointing.)  What do you say to the boy with the blindfold?  (The child answers, *You are ___ !*  Then, say,) Pretend you are at the party.  Tell me what you and your friends are doing.  (The child answers, *We are ___ .*  Next, say,) Pretend you are the boy with the blindfold.  What do you say?  (The child answers, *I am ___ .*)


**Pretest Directions:  Receptive**

Materials:  red, green, yellow, purple, and pink crayons

Let's practice listening carefully.  Look at your worksheet.  It shows children playing a game at a birthday party.  I will talk about what you see and tell you what to do on your worksheet.

1.  Listen.  Draw a red box around what I say.  He is at the party.

2.  Listen.  Draw a green box around what I say.  It has a tail.

3.  Listen.  Draw a yellow box around what I say.  She is not laughing.

4.  Listen.  Draw a purple box around your name if you are a boy.

5.  Listen.  Draw a pink box around the people who say, ''We are playing a birthday game.''

Nice listening!

**Auditory Bombardment**   Listen carefully. (Stress the pronoun in each sentence as you slowly point to each picture.)
   Here is Sam.   He is happy.
   This is Andrea.   She is tall.
   These are Andrea's friends.   They are playing.
   These are Sam's friends.   They are ice skating.

**Auditory Discrimination**   Listen to what I say. Then, point to the picture I talk about.  (Describe the pictures at random.)
   He is happy.
   She is tall.
   They are playing jumprope.
   They are ice skating.

(For the pronouns *we, I,* and *you,* roleplay.   For example, say,) Now, I'll pretend I am Andrea.   (Point to Andrea's picture and say,) I am tall.

**To Do Activity**   Cut these pictures apart and mount them on colored construction paper.   Then, make a tree without leaves out of poster board.   Have the child choose the picture you describe and paste that leaf on the tree.

195

**Auditory Bombardment**   Listen carefully.  (Stress the pronoun in each sentence as you slowly point to each picture.)

   This is a cat.   It is jumping
   Here is Sam's father.   He is driving.
   Here are some toys.   They are cars.
   These children are at school.   They are reading.

**Auditory Discrimination**   Listen to what I say.  Then, point to the picture I talk about.  (Describe the pictures at random.)

   It is jumping.
   He is driving.
   They are cars.
   They are reading.

(For the pronouns *we, I,* and *you,* roleplay.   For example, say,)  Now, let's pretend I am this boy/girl and you are that boy/girl.   (Point to one of the children ice skating and say),  We are ice skating.

**To Do Activity**   Cut these pictures apart and place them on the floor.   Have the child toss a beanbag on the picture you describe.

196

Name _____

**Sentence Repetition**   Say what I say.   (Point to each picture as you say:)

   They are laughing.
   He can't see.
   It is on the wall.
   It is sitting.

**Sentence Production**   (Point to each picture and use a wh-question prompt.   For example, ask,) Who is laughing?   (The child responds with sentences such as:)

   They are laughing.
   He can't see.
   It is on the wall.
   It is sitting.

(For the pronouns *we, I,* and *you,* roleplay with the child.   For example, say,) Pretend you are at the party. Tell me what you and your friends are doing.   (The child answers, *We* are ____ .)

**To Do Activity**   Cut these pictures apart and mount them on tagboard cards to make "letters."   Make a mailbox out of a shoebox and let the child "mail" a letter if she uses a correct sentence to describe the picture on the envelope.

SUBJECTIVE PRONOUNS

**Sentence Repetition**   Say what I say.   (Point to each picture as you say:)
   She is taking a picture.
   It is on the table.
   She is pointing.
   They are playing.

**Sentence Production**   (Point to one of the pictures and use a wh-question prompt.   For example, ask,) Who is taking a picture?   (The child responds with sentences such as:)
   She is taking a picture.
   It is on the table.
   She is pointing.
   They are playing.

(For the pronouns *we, I,* and *you,* roleplay with the child.   For example, say,) Pretend you are this girl. (Point to the girl who is pointing.)   What do you say to the boy with the blindfold?   (The child answers, *You are ___!)*

**To Do Activity**   Cut these pictures apart and mount them on the large pieces of a simple puzzle.   Have the child pick a piece and put it together with the other pieces if he describes the picture correctly.

198

**Expanded Sentence Repetition**   Say what I say.
(Point to each picture as you say:)
   They are playing soccer.
   He is trying to catch the ball.
   They are shouting at their team.
   He is holding a sign.

**Expanded Sentence Production**   (Point to each
picture and use a wh-question prompt.   For
example, ask,)  Who is playing soccer?   (The child
responds with sentences such as:)
   They are playing soccer.
   He is trying to catch the ball.
   They are shouting at their team.
   He is holding a sign.

(For the pronouns *I, we,* and *you,* roleplay with the child.   For example, say,) Pretend you are the boy
kicking the ball.   Tell me what you are doing.   (The child answers, *I am kicking the ball.*)

**To Do Activity**   Mount these pictures on cardboard and cut them apart to make individual pieces of pizza.
Let the child choose a piece, describe it using an expanded sentence, and add her pieces together to make
a whole pizza!

SUBJECTIVE PRONOUNS                      199

**Expanded Sentence Repetition**   Say what I say.
(Point to each picture as you say:)
    It is on the ground.
    They are shaking their pom-poms.
    She is wearing earmuffs.
    He has a whistle in his hand.

**Expanded Sentence Production**   (Point to each picture and use a wh-question prompt.   For example, ask,) What is on the ground?   (The child responds with expanded sentences such as:)
    It is on the ground.
    They are shaking their pom-poms.
    She is wearing earmuffs.
    He has a whistle in his hand.

(For the pronouns *I, we,* and *you,* roleplay with the child.   For example, say,) Pretend you are the woman with earmuffs.   Tell me what you are wearing.   (The child answers, *I am wearing earmuffs.*)

**To Do Activity**   Make two copies of these pictures.   Cut them apart and mount them on poster board cards. Shuffle the cards and deal them out.   Take turns drawing a card from the other person and laying down a pair after describing the picture correctly.

SUBJECTIVE PRONOUNS

**Worksheet 5: At the Soccer Game**

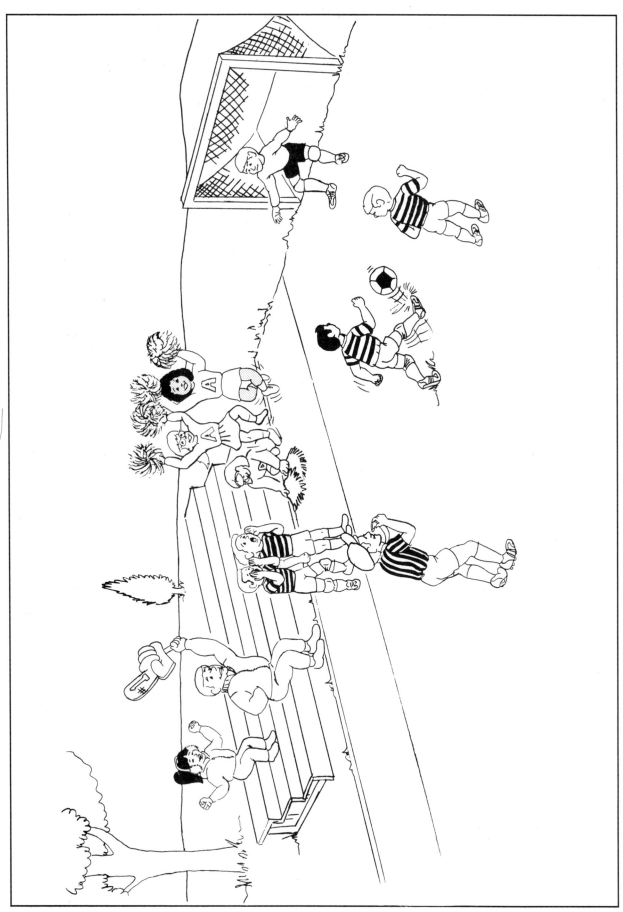

# Worksheet 5:   At the Soccer Game

## Carryover Directions

Tell me about this picture.   (If the child has difficulty, point to one of the pictures and say,) Tell me about this one.   (Continue with the task until the child uses all the subjective pronouns in sentences such as:)

1.   They are shouting at their team.

2.   He is trying to catch the ball.

3.   They are shaking their pom-poms.

4.   She is picking up her pom-pom.

5.   He is holding a sign.

6.   She is wearing earmuffs.

7.   He has a whistle in his hand.

8.   It is in his hand.

(To elicit the pronouns *I, you,* and *we,* roleplay with the child.   For example, say,) Pretend you are this boy.   (Point to the boy who is trying to catch the ball.)   What are you doing?   (The child answers, *I am trying to catch the ball.*   Next, say,) Pretend you are one of these players.   (Point to one of the players on the sidelines.)   What are you and your friends doing?   (The child answers, *We are shouting at our team.*   Next, say,) Pretend I am this woman.   (Point to the woman wearing earmuffs.)   What am I wearing?   (The child answers, *You are wearing earmuffs.*)

## To Do Activity

Make a pronoun booklet.   Write each of the pronouns (e.g., *he, she, they, it*) on the top of a page. Have the child color the pictures on his worksheet and then cut them apart.   If he can describe them correctly, let him paste them on the pages where they belong.   Also, have the child do the same with pictures he cuts out from magazines.   If desired, use photos of yourself and the child, or have the child draw pictures, for *I, you,* and *we.*

**Worksheet 6: Dinner Time**

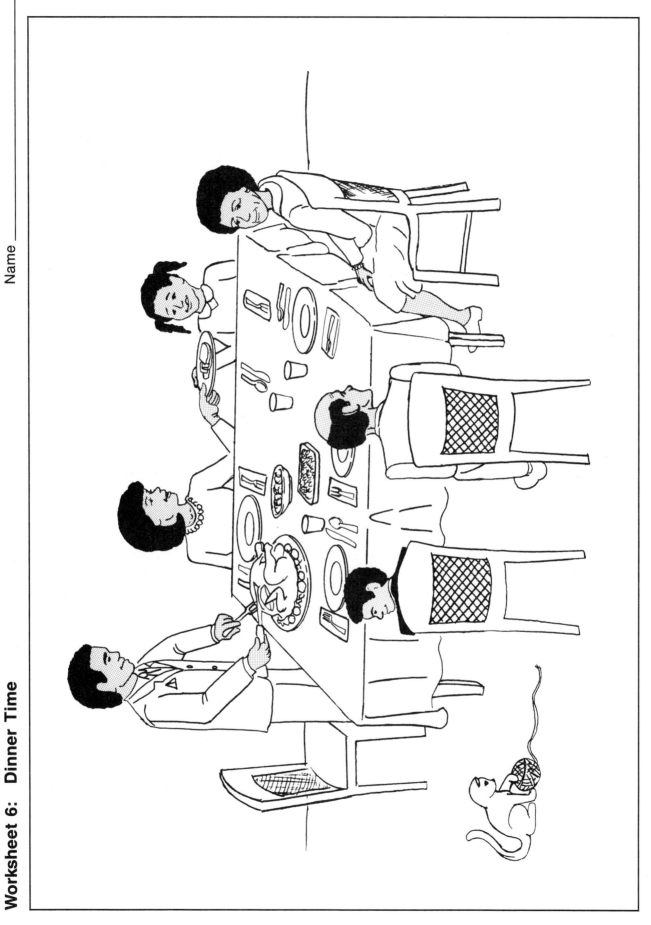

203

## Worksheet 6:  Dinner Time

**Posttest Directions**

Here are some pictures.   Tell me all about them.   (If the child has difficulty, point to one of the pictures and say,) Tell me about him/her/them/it.   (Continue until the child uses all the subjective pronouns in sentences such as:)

1.  <u>He</u> is carving the turkey.

2.  <u>She</u> is giving the plate to the girl.

3.  <u>They</u> are sitting at the table.

4.  <u>It</u> is playing with yarn.

5.  <u>He</u> is the grandpa.

6.  <u>She</u> is the grandma.

7.  <u>It</u> is a Thanksgiving turkey.

8.  <u>They</u> are the youngest in the family.

(To elicit the pronouns *I, we,* and *you,* roleplay with the child.   For example, say,) Pretend you are this girl.   (Point to the girl beside her mother.)   Where are you sitting?   (The child answers, *I am sitting beside my mother.*   Then, say,) Pretend this is your family.   What are you and your family doing?   (The child answers, <u>*We*</u> *are having dinner.*   Next, say,) Pretend I am this woman.   (Point to the mother.)   What am I doing?   (The child answers, <u>*You*</u> *are giving the plate to your daughter.*)

**To Do Activity**

Copy two sets of these pictures.   Cut one set apart.   Let the child choose an individual picture and place it on the picture it matches in the scene if she can describe it correctly.   See if she can cover up all the pictures.   For the pronouns *I, we,* and *you,* roleplay with the child.

1-2-123567